MATH That MATTERS

Targeted Assessment and
Feedback for Grades 3–8

• • • • •

Also by Marian Small

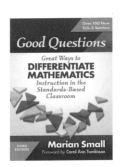

Good Questions:
Great Ways to Differentiate
Mathematics Instruction in the
Standards-Based Classroom
(3rd edition)

Fun and Fundamental
Math for Young Children:
Building a Strong Foundation
in PreK–Grade 2

Teaching Mathematical Thinking:
Tasks and Questions to Strengthen
Practices and Processes

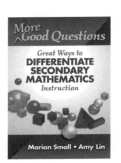

More Good Questions:
Great Ways to Differentiate
Secondary Mathematics Instruction
(with Amy Lin)

Building Proportional Reasoning
Across Grades and
Math Strands, K–8

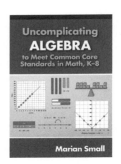

Uncomplicating Algebra
to Meet Common Core
Standards in Math, K–8

Uncomplicating Fractions
to Meet Common Core
Standards in Math, K–7

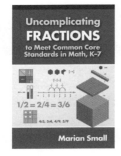

Eyes on Math:
A Visual Approach to
Teaching Math Concepts
(Illustrations by Amy Lin)

MATH That MATTERS

Targeted Assessment and Feedback for Grades 3–8

• • • • •

Marian Small

Foreword by Damian Cooper

TEACHERS COLLEGE PRESS

TEACHERS COLLEGE | COLUMBIA UNIVERSITY
NEW YORK AND LONDON

NATIONAL COUNCIL OF
TEACHERS OF MATHEMATICS
1906 Association Drive, Reston, VA 20191
www.nctm.org

Ru'bicon

Published simultaneously by Teachers College Press, 1234 Amsterdam Avenue, New York, NY 10027; National Council of Teachers of Mathematics, 1906 Association Drive, Reston, VA 20191; and Rubicon Publishing Inc., 2040 Speers Road, Oakville, Ontario L6L 2X8, Canada.

Text Design: Lynne Frost

Library of Congress Cataloging-in-Publication Data

Names: Small, Marian, author.
Title: Math that matters : targeted assessment and feedback for grades 3–8 / Marian Small ; foreword by Damian Cooper.
Other titles: Targeted assessment and feedback for grades 3–8
Description: New York, NY : Teachers College Press, [2019] | Includes bibliographical references and index. |
Identifiers: LCCN 2019000614 (print) | LCCN 2019002840 (ebook) | ISBN 9780807777794 (ebook) | ISBN 9780807761427 (pbk. : alk. paper)
Subjects: LCSH: Mathematics teachers—In-service training. | Mathematics—Study and teaching (Elementary) | Mathematics—Study and teaching (Middle school) | Elementary school teachers—In-service training. | Middle school teachers— In-service training.
Classification: LCC QA10.5 (ebook) | LCC QA10.5 .S6295 2019 (print) | DDC 372.7/044—dc23
LC record available at https://lccn.loc.gov/2019000614

ISBN 978-0-8077-6142-7 (paper)
ISBN 978-0-8077-7779-4 (ebook)
ISBN 978-0-8077-6177-9 (hardcover)

Printed on acid-free paper
Manufactured in the United States of America

· · ·

Contents

• • •

Foreword

IN MY ROLE as an education consultant, I work with teachers across all grade levels and all subjects. As one might expect, teachers attending workshops and other professional development sessions demonstrate the full range of openness with respect to changing their assessment and grading practices. And while I am extremely cautious about making generalizations as to which groups of educators are more or less open to change, I can say, definitively, that mathematics tends to be a less than fertile field when asking teachers to consider alternatives to traditional "paper-and-pencil" assessment. Similarly, the common refrain "I have so much marking to do tonight" all too often means that the teacher collects students' written responses to math problems, takes them home, and spends hours circling and correcting the errors. But in this scenario, who is doing the thinking? Certainly not the students!

When I challenge these practices and suggest that effective "assessment" goes far beyond marking and involves feedback to improve learning, reactions typically include "What would you provide feedback on in math?" or "Math is not like language arts or social studies. The answer is either right or wrong." To such reactions I suggest that numerical scoring merely indicates to a student how many answers were correct, whereas the primary purpose of assessment in all subjects, including mathematics, should be to improve skills and understanding. To do that, assessment must empower students to become reliable, autonomous monitors of their own work. In other words, effective assessment teaches students how to identify and correct their own errors—not to rely, forever, on a teacher to do that for them. Simply scoring work ensures students' dependency on the teacher. This is why assessment tools like rubrics are essential: A well-constructed rubric, more importantly than being a scoring tool, describes what quality work looks like, from novice to expert level, and thereby provides students with the information they need to improve their own learning.

When facilitating workshops, I provide numerous examples of mathematics classes in which teachers are using progressive, research-based alternative assessment strategies to improve student learning. But since the focus of my professional work for three decades has been student assessment, I always inform audiences of my own lack of expertise and formal credentials when it comes to mathematics education. (My classroom teaching was mostly in English, drama, and special education.)

And so it is an honor to write this Foreword for Marian Small's latest book, *Math That Matters: Targeted Assessment and Feedback for Grades 3–8*. Unlike me, Marian blends a deep understanding of mathematics and her years of experience as a mathematics educator with a profound grasp of current research and assessment practice. Marian's numerous publications and resources have benefited countless teachers across Canada, the United States, and internationally. Her knowledge of curriculum and instruction have helped educators and school leaders understand what is essential for students to learn, and how best to teach it. But in *Math That Matters,* Marian has completed the learning cycle by confronting the challenge of assessing learning in mathematics. No matter how well teachers understand the mathematics curriculum, or how well developed is their instructional repertoire, assessment is where "the rubber meets the road." A teacher's approach to assessment communicates to children and their parents what really "counts." Because assessment of mathematics has traditionally been more resistant to change than other curriculum areas, Marian's resource is both necessary and welcome.

Math That Matters begins with an examination of how teachers communicate what they actually value in mathematics, as reflected in the kinds of questions and prompts they present to students. In the next two chapters, Marian examines and explains fundamental principles of assessment, based on current research, and ties these principles directly to mathematics. Marian knows from experience that many teachers employ a full and appropriate range of assessment strategies and tools in their language arts, social science, and, yes, science programs. But all too often, when it comes to mathematics, assessment defaults to the tried and true: "I'll have them write a test." And so the first part of *Math That Matters* goes on to explain and illustrate that a sound, effective assessment plan for mathematics includes all of the following elements:

- Clear delineation of three purposes for assessment: diagnosing students' strengths and needs before instruction (diagnostic); improving students' skills and conceptual understanding during the learning process (formative); and determining levels of proficiency at the end of each instructional cycle (summative)
- An appropriate balance of assessment tasks addressing skills, conceptual understanding, and application of learning
- A corresponding balance of written questions, conversation with students, and observation of students during performance tasks

But it is Chapter 3 on feedback that is perhaps the most crucial. Fundamentally, effective feedback improves student self-reflection and metacognition skills that no amount of traditional marking will ever accomplish. Marian stresses that feedback is communication. And because communication is essentially about the relationship between two or more human beings, there is no one correct way to do it; it depends on the individual child. What constitutes effective feedback for one learner may be entirely ineffective for another in the same class. This chapter also explains six distinct types of feedback and examines critical variables including timing of feedback and anticipation of common errors.

In the second part of *Math That Matters,* Marian provides grade- and strand-specific explanations of what effective assessment looks like for Grades 3 through 8, with each chapter modeling the assessment principles discussed in the first part of the book. Each of these chapters includes examples of how to assess skills and conceptual understanding, as well as opportunities for the application of mathematical skills and understanding through performance tasks. And to assist teachers in implementing a rich, balanced approach to assessment, Marian includes not only sample questions but also rubrics and checklists.

Our understanding of the power of assessment to improve learning has deepened significantly in the past two decades. In *Math That Matters: Targeted Assessment and Feedback for Grades 3–8,* Marian Small draws upon the critical research behind this understanding to explain what effective practice looks like. It is essential reading for all elementary educators and has the potential to profoundly affect the quality of mathematics assessment in our schools.

—Damian Cooper
President, Plan Teach Assess Consulting
Past-President, The Canadian Assessment
for Learning Network, CAfLN

• • •

Preface

ASSESSMENT is the process of gathering information that can be used to make decisions. In the world of education, large-scale assessment (i.e., standardized state, national, or international testing) is used to inform systems, and classroom-based assessment is used to monitor and guide the learning of individual students in a particular classroom.

Although large-scale assessment is an important (and generally unavoidable) feature of education, this resource focuses on classroom-based assessment, which impacts students as individuals on an almost-daily basis. A teacher might gather assessment data for any of the following reasons:

- As an informal check on whether a particular student has grasped a particular idea to guide further instruction
- As an informal check on whether a particular student holds a certain misconception that would need to be addressed
- As an informal check to see whether a particular student needs to be pushed farther or moved to a different learning situation better suited to his or her individual abilities
- As a formal check on whether a particular student has mastered a particular standard for reporting purposes

Feedback is the process of reacting to student work, whether written work, an oral response, or a performance. Feedback can be evaluative, a nonevaluative comment, or a further question for probing or scaffolding.

WHAT DO I MEAN BY *ASSESSMENT* IN THIS RESOURCE?

This resource focuses, in equal parts, on assessment *for* learning and assessment *of* learning. Assessment for learning involves collecting or considering data related to student thinking and performance, and serves purposes other than assigning grades or marks. Assessment of learning generally involves collecting data related to student thinking and performance, for purposes of reporting—to the system, to parents, or to both. I also address assessment *as* learning, focused on self-assessment, in this resource.

WHAT CONSTITUTES FEEDBACK?

This resource explores feedback less as marking student responses as correct or incorrect, and more as providing comments or questions addressing a variety of issues, such as choice of strategy, choice of perspective, level of creativity, the need to extend, and so forth. Good feedback helps students self-regulate and self-assess.

WHAT IS SPECIAL ABOUT THIS BOOK?

This book is unique in several ways.

It differs from other books on assessment in mathematics in its emphasis on development of a standards-based full assessment plan including both formative and summative assessment.

It is not just theoretical and not just a set of provided questions. Attention is focused on both theories of assessment and specific math content. The attention to content ensures that readers are provided with more insight into purpose when creating assessment questions. The book is notable also for the number of suggested assessment questions provided at many grade levels and in many content domains.

It is different, as well, in providing deeper attention than many assessment resources to feedback as an important component of the assessment process, with detail on types of feedback in math and illustrations of the application of feedback.

ORGANIZATION OF THE BOOK

This book is organized into three main sections. The first three chapters lay the theoretical groundwork for an exploration of assessment. Chapter 1 focuses on the fundamental principle that recognizing that the math we think matters always informs our instructional and assessment decisions. Chapter 2 focuses on foundational ideas in assessment, both formative and summative. Chapter 3 focuses on foundational ideas about feedback.

The next six chapters illustrate sample applications of the theory in a variety of areas of math. Chapters 4–9 provide significant detail on full assessment plans for each of Grades 3–8 in one of six content domains as exemplified by a commonly used set of standards (Common Core State Standards Initiative [CCSSI], 2010). Even teachers who follow a different set of standards will find the content they teach.

Finally, Chapter 10 summarizes the key walk-away points.

DIFFERENTIATED ASSESSMENT

This resource carries on previous work I have done on differentiating instruction. Many of the suggested questions allow for differentiated responses. It also carries on my continuing work in clarifying the important math ideas that should underlie instruction in the domains that are explored.

Any 3rd-grade to 8th-grade teacher could benefit from studying the content domain illustrated at his or her own grade level, but looking at a different grade in a domain of interest can also be very useful. Many of the ideas presented are transportable to other grade levels. It might have been nice to have examined every domain at every grade level, but such a resource would have quickly become unwieldy.

My intention throughout this resource is to help teachers see what assessment and feedback focused on the ideas and relationships underlying the standards, rather than just skills, can look like. This type of assessment encourages teachers and students alike to focus on thinking and problem solving, rather than just procedures. Such learning will serve students well beyond the classroom.

Acknowledgments

SO MUCH of what I have been able to produce is a result of my long experience working with teachers. I thank all of them, whether they are in New Brunswick, where I began this work; in Winnipeg, where I have been in classrooms in the last few years; or in Ontario, where so many teachers have had me into their classrooms.

In particular, I thank the teachers who helped me gather the samples presented in this book. This work was supported by several coaches and consultants whom I would particularly like to acknowledge: Tracy Joyce, in Renfrew Catholic District School Board; Peggy-Sue Fox, in Bluewater School District; and Ann Arden, in Ottawa Carlton District School Board.

Some of the ideas about focusing on feedback came about because of the lovely invitation from Anastasiya Lipnevich at Queens University to write a chapter on feedback in mathematics for a handbook on feedback she was co-editing. Her invitation encouraged me to think more deeply about the connection between assessment and feedback and to incorporate those ideas in this book. Her co-editor, Jeffrey Smith, helped me clarify my thinking on feedback, and I acknowledge him as well.

It has been a great pleasure to work, again, with the excellent professionals at Teachers College Press to create another math resource that we hope teachers will find useful. In particular, I thank Jean Ward, Lynne Frost, and Karl Nyberg.

MATH That MATTERS

Targeted Assessment and
Feedback for Grades 3–8

• • • • •

• CHAPTER 1 •

Linking Assessment and Feedback
to Learning Goals

WHAT TEACHERS choose to assess or comment on can vary from one teacher to the next. While some teachers focus on what was wrong, others focus on what was right. While some teachers assess whether students have met standards minimally, others want to know whether students can deal with more complex situations. While some teachers focus on whether students do as they were shown, others focus on whether students can create their own strategies.

Nobody can say which focus is right or which is wrong, but the position a teacher takes on classroom-based assessment reflects deeply that teacher's beliefs about what matters in math and what his or her learning goals really are.

HOW ASSESSMENT AND FEEDBACK REFLECT OUR VALUES

When looking at the learning standards for any jurisdiction, a teacher needs to interpret their intent. Sometimes teachers use a textbook and allow the author of that book to interpret for them, but someone must make sense of what is required of a student based on a particular learning standard.

It might be assumed that the requirements are obvious and that there is nothing to interpret, but while perhaps there are instances where that is so, in most cases, interpretation is essential.

For example, consider this standard:

> Use addition and subtraction within 100 to solve one- and two-step word problems involving situations of adding to, taking from, putting together, taking apart, and comparing with unknowns in all positions, e.g., by using drawings and equations with a symbol for the unknown number to represent the problem.
>
> (CCSSI, 2010)

A teacher has to decide:

- Does it have to be any numbers or would the standard be achieved if students could do this with lots of, but not all, numbers?

- Does a student have to show both steps in what the teacher perceives as a two-step word problem? What if a student does one of the steps implicitly?
- What if a student can solve the problems but is not good with the symbol representing the unknown? How important is that?
- Do the problems have to be word problems or can they be presented visually (e.g., in a video or illustration) or as a mix?
- How complex should the problems be?

The teacher's beliefs about the intention of the standard will be reflected in his or her assessment strategies and in the feedback he or she gives.

WHAT DOES THIS LOOK LIKE (MORE SPECIFICALLY)?

Let's look at some specific examples of how teachers might make extremely different assessment decisions based on the same standards.

Grade 3 Measurement and Data

Consider, for example, this standard:

> Determine the solutions to problems involving addition and subtraction of time intervals in minutes using pictorial models or tools such as a 15-minute event plus a 30-minute event equals 45 minutes.
>
> (Texas Education Agency, 2015)

What choices do teachers have about what to assess?
A teacher (Teacher 1) might assess skills by asking questions like these:

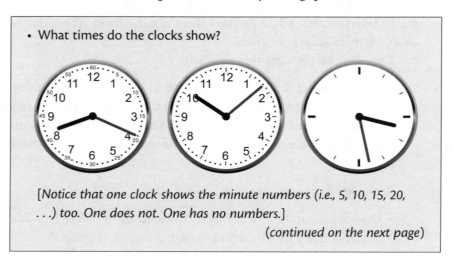

- What times do the clocks show?

[Notice that one clock shows the minute numbers (i.e., 5, 10, 15, 20, . . .) too. One does not. One has no numbers.]

(continued on the next page)

- How long did dinner last if it started at 6:18 p.m. and ended at 6:52 p.m.?
- Use a number line to show how many minutes there are between 5:37 p.m. and 7:15 p.m.

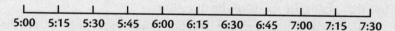

5:00 5:15 5:30 5:45 6:00 6:15 6:30 6:45 7:00 7:15 7:30

[Notice that this teacher made a decision to show a number line, ready-made, with the appropriate interval marked on it. She or he could have expected the child to come up with the line or at least the times to put on the line.]

Another teacher (Teacher 2) might focus on ideas or generalizations related to the standard, rather than on the skills, by asking questions like these:

- The minute hand of a clock and the hour hand are about a quarter of a clock apart. What time might it be?
- Jeffrey says that the amount of time between 6:18 and 6:52 could be either 34 minutes or 12 hours 34 minutes or 24 hours 34 minutes. Is he right? Are there other possibilities too? What are they?
- Lia figures out the time between 4:37 and 5:12 like this:

$$\begin{array}{r} \overset{4\ \ 10}{\cancel{5}\,\cancel{1}\,{}^{1}2} \\ -\ 4\ 3\ 7 \\ \hline 7\ 5 \end{array}$$

Do you agree with her method? Explain why or why not.

- Kyle used the number line below to figure out how many minutes passed between two times.

+21   +37

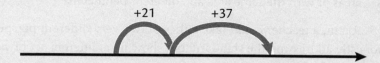

What might the times have been? Why do you think those were the times? How did the number line help?

Think about how very different the two sets of questions are.

The teacher using the first set of questions (Teacher 1) is definitely addressing the standard, but the focus is on "doing" the math. The teacher using the second set of questions is telling the students (and parents) that he or she values students seeing the bigger picture, embedding the skills inside those bigger picture questions.

The first question for Teacher 2 addresses the concept that the hands of the clock can be the same distance apart at many different times. In the course of answering this question, students will need to be specific about reading a clock, but that is not the focus of the question.

The second question for Teacher 2 addresses the notion that there is some ambiguity when we give a start time and an end time and ask for the elapsed time unless we are quite specific about whether the times are a.m. or p.m. and about the dates on which those times occurred. Students can show that they realize that the possible answers have to be 12 hours apart since we use a 12-hour clock. Students will still calculate elapsed times.

The third question for Teacher 2 ensures that students can explain how standard subtraction (based on a place value system where units differ by a factor of 10) does not apply in many situations where elapsed time is being calculated (based on a time system where units differ by a factor of 60).

The fourth question for Teacher 2 determines whether students have generalized the notion that to figure out elapsed time, a sensible approach is to "add up" in pieces, using o'clock (or other simple) benchmarks.

The two teachers' different beliefs lead to different assessments. It is entirely possible that some students who succeed in one situation might not succeed in the other. It is not that one or the other teacher is right or wrong, but information about whether a student has met the standard might not be as clear-cut as the teacher believes.

Consider another Grade 3 Measurement and Data standard:

> Solve real world and mathematical problems involving perimeters of polygons, including finding the perimeter given the side lengths, finding an unknown side length, and exhibiting rectangles with the same perimeter and different areas or with the same area and different perimeters.   (CCSSI, 2010)

Again, a teacher could take either of two very different perspectives, each one honestly addressing the standard, but showing a different set of values on the part of the teacher.

Teacher 1 might ask:

- What is the perimeter of each shape?

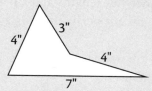 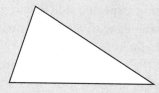

[Notice that in one instance students have to measure, but in the other they just need to show they know what a perimeter is.]
- What is the missing side length if the perimeter is 23 inches?

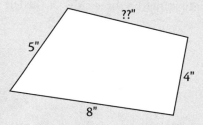

- Two rectangles with different areas have a perimeter of 30 cm. Draw what they might be. Show their lengths and widths.
- Two rectangles with different perimeters each have an area of 20 square inches. Draw the two rectangles. Show their lengths and widths.

But Teacher 2 might use a very different set of questions to assess the same standard:

- Without using specific examples, explain how you know that it must be possible for a 3-sided shape and a 5-sided shape to have the same perimeter.
- You are determining the perimeter of a quadrilateral. How many sides would you actually have to measure to figure out that perimeter?
- You know that the perimeter of an isosceles triangle is 25". If one side length is 10", what could the other side lengths be?
- Why does it make sense that if you know the perimeter of a rectangle, you don't automatically know its area?

Again, the first teacher is addressing the skills associated with the standard, whether it is determining a specific perimeter given specific side lengths, determining a specific side length given other side lengths and a perimeter, or creating rectangles with a specific area, but different perimeters, or a specific perimeter, with different areas.

The second teacher is addressing the standards from a very different perspective. He or she is looking at a bigger picture.

The first question for Teacher 2 addresses the possibility that students have generalized the notion that a perimeter is a total length that can be easily rearranged to make shapes with different numbers of sides. For example, the shape at the left can be changed to the shape at the right by using a string to build the first one and then readjusting the three sides at the left and bottom to become only two sides.

The second and third questions for Teacher 2 address the notion that having information about particular shapes can change the number of independent measurements that need to be taken. For example, to determine the perimeter of a square, only one side needs to be measured, but to determine the perimeter of an irregular quadrilateral, more sides would need to be measured. Similarly, if you know the triangle is isosceles, and you know its perimeter, you can ascertain at least one of the other side lengths (assuming you know which two sides are equal in length) without measuring it.

The fourth question for Teacher 2 concentrates on the generalization that area and perimeter are independent measures of a rectangle.

Grade 5 Number and Operations—Fractions

Looking at another grade and another topic, the same situation is evident. Different teachers can make very different decisions about the intention of the standard.

Consider this standard:

> Interpret a fraction as a division of the numerator by the denominator. Solve word problems involving division of whole numbers leading to answers in the form of fractions or mixed numbers, e.g., by using visual fraction models or equations to represent the problem.   (CCSSI, 2010)

Any teacher assessing students on this standard will need to address the fact that $a \div b = \frac{a}{b}$, but whether the teacher asks students to prove they understand why that is the case is up to the teacher.

One teacher might assess students on the standard with questions like these:

> • Write $\frac{12}{3}$ as a division.
> • Write $14 \div 5$ as a fraction or mixed number.
> • Use a picture or an equation to solve this problem: Three pies are being divided up into 4 equal portions. How big will each portion be?

A different teacher might assess with questions like these:

> • Draw a picture that shows why $15 \div 4 = 3\frac{3}{4}$.
> • Draw a picture to show why $4 \div 5 = \frac{4}{5}$.
> • Create a problem that is solved by dividing two whole numbers where the solution is $\frac{2}{3}$.

The second teacher is showing that he or she values *why* something is true and not just *how* to arrive at an answer. Note that asking a student to draw a picture to show an idea is often a meaningful way for the student to show understanding. Similarly, the creation of a problem is often a way to show understanding.

Or consider another Grade 5 standard on fractions:

The student will . . . solve single-step practical problems involving multiplication of a whole number, limited to 12 or less, and a proper fraction, with models.   (Virginia Department of Education, 2016)

One teacher might assess students on this standard by asking questions like these:

> • $\frac{2}{3}$ of the 12 cookies Dad baked were left on the plate. How many cookies were left? Draw a picture to show this.
> • $\frac{3}{5}$ of the 10 pizzas were vegetarian. How many pizzas were vegetarian? Use a model to explain your answer.
> • $\frac{5}{12}$ of all of the eggs in 2 egg cartons were broken. Draw a picture to show how many eggs were broken.

But another teacher might use a task like this instead:

A problem about cookies is solved by drawing this picture:

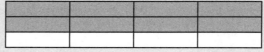

- What might the problem have been?
- How does the model help you see that multiplication is involved?
- What other picture might have been used to solve the same problem?

Notice that the first teacher's questions require solving simple practical problems involving multiplication of a whole number by a proper fraction, as well as use of a picture or a model. But the second teacher's task goes a bit farther by asking students to recognize what kinds of situations a particular visual might help explain and why.

Grade 7 Ratios and Proportional Relationships

The fact that teacher beliefs about what matters in math affect the nature of assessment is as true in higher grades as in lower grades.

Consider this standard:

Compute unit rates associated with ratios of fractions, including ratios of lengths, areas, and other quantities measured in like or different units.

(CCSSI, 2010)

One teacher might assess students on this standard by asking questions such as these:

- If a person paints $\frac{2}{3}$ of a wall in $\frac{3}{4}$ of an hour, how many walls can he paint in 1 hour?
- Write a unit rate to describe $\frac{2}{5}$ mile in each $\frac{2}{3}$ of an hour.

Another teacher might ask:

- Describe $\frac{1}{2}$ mile in $\frac{2}{3}$ of an hour using many different unit rates.

The second teacher is focusing students on the idea that there are automatically at least two unit rates describing any rate (e.g., 60 miles/hour is also $\frac{1}{60}$ hour/mile) but that with unit changes there could be many other unit rates (e.g., 1 minute/mile or 60 seconds/mile), which is a broader generalization.

Or consider another standard:

Solve problems involving ratios, rates, and percents, including multi-step problems involving percent increase and percent decrease, and financial literacy problems.
(Texas Education Agency, 2015)

Teacher 1 might assess students on this standard by using questions like these:

> - A dress that originally cost $50 was marked down 25% and then marked down 40% off the reduced price. How much did it finally cost?
> - A restaurant added 8% tax on a $36 bill. Then the client paid an 18% tip. How much did the client pay?

But Teacher 2 might add or focus on questions like these:

> - A price was increased by a total of 20% in two stages. The second increase was a percent increase based on the first increase. What could the two percent increases have been?
> - A price was reduced by x%. What does that price have to be increased by to go back to the original amount? Why is it NOT x%?

Notice that both questions from Teacher 2 focus on generalizations. The first brings out the concept that there are many ways to get a two-step increase of 20% (e.g., 5% and then 14.3%, or 10% and then 9.1%, or 2% and then 17.6%) and that the two increases together always add to less than 20%). The second requires students to realize that the increase is based on a smaller whole than the original that was decreased, and so the increase has to be more than x% to get back to the original whole (e.g., decrease by 5% and then increase by 5.26% or decrease by 10% and then increase by 11.1%).

SUMMARY

This chapter has examined the extremely important idea that a teacher's classroom-based assessment and feedback reflect a teacher's beliefs, whether conscious or unconscious, about what aspects of mathematics or particular standards in mathematics really matter. Beyond ideas about what specific content might be addressed, these beliefs affect the focus on the relative importance of skills and procedures versus concepts.

• CHAPTER 2 •

Assessment for Learning, as Learning, and of Learning

EDUCATORS often recognize two types of assessment data: assessment *for* learning and assessment *of* learning. Sometimes a third type is identified as well: assessment *as* learning (Black & Wiliam, 2018). The focus in collecting data for assessment for learning is to inform a teacher's subsequent interactions with students. Assessment as learning focuses on students' own awareness of their knowledge and understanding. Assessment of learning is what is traditionally called evaluation and measures a student's knowledge after teaching of a topic has been completed. This chapter discusses each of these forms of assessment in depth.

ASSESSMENT FOR LEARNING

Assessment for learning has been found to be an essential part of successful learning (Guskey, 2003). This form of assessment allows teachers to use data gathered to alter instruction in ways that are more likely to help move students along the learning path they need. Within assessment for learning—sometimes called formative assessment—there is often attention to diagnostic assessment, that is, data collected prior to any instructional situation to ascertain where students already stand in that area of study.

Many other types of formative assessment may be conducted during instruction. Some types are formalized and named, such as round robin charts, exit tickets, four corners, observations, interviews, "show me," hinge questions, and so forth (National Council of Teachers of English, 2013; Fennell, McCord Kobett, & Wray, 2017). But, in general, formative assessment is really about teachers listening to what students say and do and thinking about how that should influence instruction. Another form of formative assessment—student response to feedback—is discussed in more depth in Chapter 3.

Illustrative examples of formative assessments are included in the discussion that follows. Many other examples of data collection for formative assessment and how the data might be used are described for a range of content domains and grades in Chapters 4–9.

Diagnostic Assessment

Diagnostic assessment is conducted to gather data prior to instruction to determine either whether students have the prerequisite skills deemed as essential for the new learning or whether they already know what a teacher is planning to teach. In the former case, if students are found lacking in prerequisite skills, the teacher may need to go back to re-teach ideas essential to further progress. In the latter case, if students already know the planned material, the teacher might decide to skip what was planned, either for individual students, for small groups of students, or possibly (but less often) for the entire group. Many organizations and publishers have created diagnostic assessment tools, such as Leaps and Bounds (Small, Crofoot, & Lin, 2011), First Steps in Mathematics (Department of Education Western Australia, 2013), and Mathematics Initial Assessment—Elementary (Ontario Ministry of Education, 2011).

A diagnostic assessment requires a teacher to consider what pieces of knowledge are deemed as real prerequisites and not necessarily just nice-to-haves. He or she might also need to pin down the most critical prerequisites rather than every possible prerequisite to make the assessment more manageable. This sometimes involves looking at the curriculum from the previous grade, or sometimes more than one grade back; sometimes, prerequisite content has been taught earlier in the same grade. It is possible that a teacher will address standards of mathematical practice in this diagnosis, but, more likely, the focus will be on aspects of content.

Sometimes the diagnostic assessment is conducted with a single task, and at other times it might be something more like a quiz, where many separate pieces are explored. In either case, a teacher must decide on what needs to be checked, whether skills (procedures) or concepts or both.

Consider, for example, two situations that are described below: a diagnostic assessment relevant to teaching a Grade 4 topic on multiplication and division of whole numbers and a diagnostic relevant to teaching a Grade 7 topic on 2-dimensional area of polygons and volume and surface area of right prisms.

Grade 4 Multiplication and Division of Whole Numbers

To successfully deal with this topic, a student certainly needs to know the multiplication facts and also must know how to multiply a single-digit number by a multiple of 10 or 100 or 1000. He or she also needs to know the relationship between multiplication and division, have some familiarity with situations in which these operations are applied, and, in the case of division, understand the concept of a remainder.

A teacher might get at these ideas by setting up a series of questions or might create a single task to assess readiness to proceed.

A Series of Questions

1. ☐ × ☐ is between 20 and 30. What could the two numbers be?
2. A number in the 40s is divided by a 1-digit number. The answer has no remainder. What could the division be?
3. You divide a 2-digit number by a 1-digit number and the quotient (the answer) is the same as the divisor (what you divided by). What could the division have been?
4. Draw a picture to show why 4 × 30 has to be a whole number that ends in 0.
5. Write two problems:
   a. One that could be solved by multiplying 5 × 20
   b. One that could be solved by dividing 140 by 4
6. You do a division and the remainder is 5. What do you know about what numbers you might have divided?

Questions 1–3 above assess specific skills in a succinct fashion. Questions 4–6 address concepts and require more involved answers. A diagnostic is most useful if it addresses both skills and concepts.

A Single Task

Instead of a series of questions, a teacher might decide to use a single task as a diagnostic assessment. For example:

Create two different problems you could solve by dividing a 3-digit number by a 1-digit number, but where there is a remainder in completing one division but not the other.
- Do not divide by the same amount both times.
- Solve both problems.
- Tell how you could have solved each by multiplying instead.

Note that the series of questions illustrated earlier addressed some prerequisites that this task does not, but the payoff here is a "quicker" task, or at least one that may be perceived as less onerous by students because there are fewer parts.

The two assessments just discussed focus on prerequisite knowledge for a planned course of teaching. If instead a teacher wants to use a diagnostic tool to see if students already know the ideas that are about to be taught, the diagnostic would have to look quite different. In this case, it would focus on the planned new knowledge—multiplication and division involving 4-digit and 1-digit numbers—but would still address the meanings of multiplication and division and the meaning of a remainder in division.

Grade 7 Area and Volume

To successfully deal with this topic, a student certainly needs to know what area and volume mean, to be able to determine areas of rectangles and triangles, and to be able to determine the areas and volumes of rectangular right prisms. Again, a teacher might use a series of questions or might use a single task.

A Series of Questions

1. Draw a sketch with dimensions shown as an example of:
   a. a shape with an area of 12 square units
   b. a shape with a volume of 15 cubic units
2. A rectangle and a triangle each have an area of 20 square units. Draw 2 possible rectangles and 2 possible triangles.
3. A rectangular prism has a base of 20 square units. What do you know about the prism if:
   a. the volume is 10 cubic units?
   b. the volume is 35 cubic units?
   c. the height is 6 units?

A Single Task

- Choose a 2-digit number.
- Create a rectangle and a triangle with that area.
- Create a rectangular prism with a volume a little less than that number of cubic units.
- Now do the same with a mixed number instead of your original 2-digit number.

A teacher might decide not to worry about fractions in this context and leave out the part about the mixed number, on the grounds that it is not a critical prerequisite for area and volume determinations.

If a teacher wants to use a diagnostic to determine whether students already know the ideas that will be taught, the diagnostic would be different, focusing on determining the area of a variety of polygons and the surface area and volume of a variety of polygonal right prisms.

Formal Versus Informal Formative Assessment

Most educators agree that formative assessment is essential to identify different students' learning needs and modify instruction appropriately. Black and Wiliam (2009) suggest that the point of gathering formative assessment evidence is to make better instructional decisions than could be made without gathering that evidence. Earl (2003) asserts that teachers gather good evidence only by both knowing their students and knowing the curriculum.

Sometimes a task is deliberately set for the purpose of gathering formative assessment, but at other times information just comes out in a learning situation that was not created particularly for the purpose of collecting data. For example, a 3rd-grade teacher might set a task like the one below to gather formative information about student mastery of the associative property of multiplication (i.e., that $a \times (b \times c) = (a \times b) \times c$):

> Are all of these statements true or are some of them lies?
> a. To multiply a number by 6, you can always multiply half of it by 3.
> b. To multiply a number by 4, you can sometimes multiply its double by 2.
> c. To multiply a number by 5, you can always multiply half of it by 10.

But informal situations can also provide formative assessment data. For example, if a teacher asks students to multiply 12 by 8 and a student says it would be easier to multiply 12 by 4 and then take half, the teacher would realize that this individual has a problem with an understanding of multiplicative relationships, and the associative property in particular.

An 8th-grade teacher might set a task like the one below to gather formative information about student mastery of the concept of irrational numbers:

> Are all of these statements true or are some of them lies?
> a. $\sqrt{35}$ is irrational since 35 is not a perfect square.
> b. Every square root is irrational.
> c. The decimal 0.444 . . . (4 keeps repeating) is irrational since it goes on forever.

Again, informal situations can also provide formative assessment data. For example, if a teacher asks students to create an irrational number with a value close to 20, and a student says that the answer has to be the square root of a whole number (which happens not to be true), the teacher would know that he or she needs to acquaint that student with other irrational numbers, for example, multiples of π.

Quizzes

Many teachers view quizzes as formative assessment. Clearly, a teacher gains information from any piece of work from a student, including a quiz, but there can be a stigma attached to quizzes. Whether we tell students that the quiz does or does not count, Belanger and Allingham (2004) suggest that if a mark is put on the quiz, students might well then ignore any other provided feedback. A high mark might lead students to overrate themselves and a low mark to underrate themselves, especially if the quiz is in any way different from the final assessment of learning. I argue in subsequent chapters that not marking work viewed as formative assessment and perhaps even avoiding the word "quiz" altogether might be a good choice.

What About Mathematical Practice Standards?

As part of assessment of all types, teachers should collect data relating to standards for mathematical practice and not just standards for content. One commonly used set of standards for mathematical practice (CCSSI, 2010) calls for a focus on evidence that

- students persevere in solving problems,
- students' reasoning is strong,
- students construct viable arguments,
- students use mathematics to model real situations,
- students use tools strategically,
- students recognize when precision is called for,
- students look for structure and use it in solving problems, and
- students look for regularity.

ASSESSMENT AS LEARNING

The more students can self-assess, the more likely they will eventually be successful learners (Andrade & Valtcheva, 2009). By being able to measure their own understanding, students can more easily make adjustments to their actions. To do this, however, students must recognize what teachers view as success. Whether this is communicated explicitly or more implicitly, students need to be aware of what it is their teachers value. This relates, of course, to what was discussed in Chapter 1, about teachers deciding and communicating what aspects of student learning they value.

Focusing on Detail or Not

However teachers choose to communicate their measures of success—whether through success criteria, rubrics, or grades—they make decisions about whether success is more about overall performance or the extent to which details matter.

For example, if teachers communicate to students that in performing calculations, they expect "everything" to be right, that is a very different message from communicating that they can live with small errors. Teachers might communicate whether they expect computations to be done in a certain way or if only particular ways are considered successful (usually termed as "efficient"). They could communicate whether they demand success on any calculation of a particular sort, no matter how complicated, or only in more straightforward situations.

How a student judges how successful he or she has been will be based on those explicit or implicit communications.

Focusing on Answer Versus Process

Many teachers will suggest that they communicate to their students that it is the process that they really care about as much as, if not more than, the solution. But their comments, success criteria, rubric descriptors, or marking scheme is more likely what students will attend to when self-assessing.

For example, if a rubric indicates that a good plan for solving a problem without the solution leads to only a level 2 on a 4-point scale, it will be hard for students to believe that the process is the focus. If most of the success criteria focus on answers, the same would be true. As they create, or co-create with students, rubrics or success criteria, teachers need to consider what students will read into them as they self-assess.

Learning to Self-Assess

Once a teacher has communicated his or her general views on measures of success in learning math (more vs. less detail, answer vs. process), students must be taught how to self-assess. There are a number of tools they can use to build assessment-as-learning knowledge, and they need to practice these techniques with peer and teacher support. Although some students will catch on quickly, others will need a lot of practice in learning how to self-assess in math. Techniques include success criteria, rubrics, samples, and self-assessment templates.

Success Criteria

Success criteria are defined as an indication of what a teacher or the teacher and students agree is essential for successful completion of a task. Explicit statements of these criteria have been judged to be very valuable for student learning (Beesley, Clark, Dempsey, & Tweed, 2018). As described above, success criteria might be more or less focused on detail or more or less focused on solutions.

Success criteria might be very generic, for example:

- Communicate in a clear and convincing way.
- Show your understanding by showing your work.
- Check your work.

Criteria such as these, however, require students to have the background knowledge of expectations to understand what clear and convincing looks like, what it means to show understanding, and whether the checking needs to be spelled out in great detail or not.

Or criteria might be much more specific, as related to a particular task, for example:

- Determine three different equivalent fractions for each given one.
- Prove that the fractions really are equivalent.

Here, too, students need some background to know what is perceived as proof and whether any three equivalent fractions are OK or not.

In subsequent chapters, I argue that there needs to be a mix of success criteria. Some should be specific and remind students of what needs to be attended to, specifically, to complete a task. And others should focus on generalizations or essential understandings students come to as a result of engaging in learning tasks.

Regardless, once students understand how to interpret success criteria, they can be immensely useful for self-assessment.

Rubrics

Rubrics, too, can be generic or specific. A generic rubric related to communication in math is illustrated on the next page. Although such a rubric might ultimately be used to support a teacher in arriving at assessment-of-learning data, it also helps students develop self-assessment as a learning strategy. If students have access to a rubric of this sort, reading the columns for Levels 3 and 4 will give them a sense of what is expected of them in terms of communication.

MATHEMATICAL COMMUNICATION				
	Level 1	**Level 2**	**Level 3**	**Level 4**
Categories	The student	The student	The student	The student
Language and organization of ideas	• is somewhat unclear in expressing thinking; the organization seems somewhat muddled	• organizes and expresses some, but not all, of the thinking appropriately	• organizes and expresses thinking appropriately	• organizes and expresses thinking with particular clarity
Recognition of audience	• seems not to consider audience in the communication used	• communicates appropriately, but only to a limited extent, for the given audience	• communicates appropriately for the given audience	• communicates particularly effectively for the given audience
Recognition of purpose	• seems not to consider purpose in the communication used	• communicates appropriately, but only to a limited extent, for the given purpose	• communicates appropriately for the given purpose	• communicates particularly effectively for the given purpose
Appropriate use of: • terminology • symbols • conventions	• is somewhat ineffective in using appropriate mathematical terminology and symbolism and in respecting mathematical conventions	• sometimes, but not always, uses appropriate mathematical terminology and symbolism and respects mathematical conventions	• appropriately uses mathematical terminology and symbolism and respects mathematical conventions	• uses mathematical terminology and symbolism with particular effectiveness and respects mathematical conventions
Communication of ideas: • orally • visually • in written explanation	• communicates somewhat ineffectively, whether in oral, visual, or written form	• communicates reasonably appropriately in oral and/or visual form, but struggles with written form	• communicates appropriately in oral, visual, or written form, as requested	• communicates clearly and effectively chooses oral, visual, or written approaches

Sometimes rubrics are much more specific. For example, a rubric can be developed that applies directly to the following task:

> • Imagine a fast food children's box.
> • Decide what the size of that box is and what its capacity is.
> • How many of those boxes could you fit into our classroom if they are put together as tightly as possible?

The task-specific rubric might be:

Criteria	Level 1 The student	Level 2 The student	Level 3 The student	Level 4 The student
Solving the two problems posed	• struggles to determine the volume of the box; errors are made	• determines the volumes of the room and the box with some errors	• correctly determines the volumes of the room and the box	• correctly determines the number of boxes that fit in the room using appropriate unit conversions
Explaining the strategies	• describes few of the processes used	• describes some of the processes used	• reasonably thoroughly describes the processes used	• insightfully describes the processes used, including making sense of the values calculated

Having access to a rubric, whether it is co-created by the student and teacher or simply provided by the teacher, helps students know what success looks like. Clearly, co-creation of rubrics goes farther in giving students insight into what constitutes success than simply handing them a rubric.

Samples

Evaluating the work of others can be beneficial in helping students develop a better sense of what is expected for work to be considered of high quality. This can be done by providing samples of work, whether good work or poor work, and allowing students to confer with partners to assess the work. Group discussion can make the process even more productive.

Of course, rather than using the work of actual students in the class, it is best to use "anonymous" work so that no personal feelings are involved.

A simplified approach to using samples involves incorporating a theoretical student's work into a task itself: "Student X solved a problem in a particular way. Explain why you agree or disagree with that approach." This prompts the student to evaluate the correctness and quality of the theoretical student's work.

Self-Assessment Templates

Teachers might use templates of various sorts to help students self-assess. Sometimes, students are asked to rate themselves on either attitude, content, or standards for practice on a point scale (e.g., 3 points, 5 points, or some other number of points). Assessment items for a template might include:

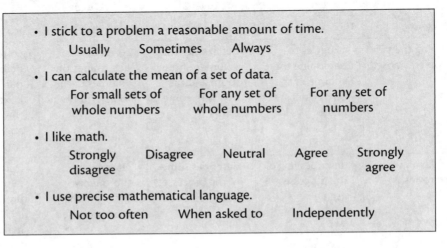

- I stick to a problem a reasonable amount of time.
  - Usually   Sometimes   Always
- I can calculate the mean of a set of data.
  - For small sets of   For any set of   For any set of
  - whole numbers   whole numbers   numbers
- I like math.
  - Strongly   Disagree   Neutral   Agree   Strongly
  - disagree   agree
- I use precise mathematical language.
  - Not too often   When asked to   Independently

Alternatively, the same sorts of issues could be addressed on a point scale, such as this one:

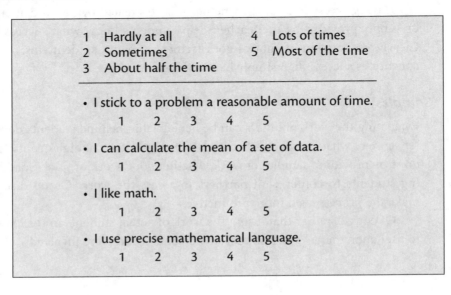

1	Hardly at all		4	Lots of times
2	Sometimes		5	Most of the time
3	About half the time			

- I stick to a problem a reasonable amount of time.
  - 1   2   3   4   5
- I can calculate the mean of a set of data.
  - 1   2   3   4   5
- I like math.
  - 1   2   3   4   5
- I use precise mathematical language.
  - 1   2   3   4   5

Sometimes full templates are provided for students to use on a regular basis (e.g., for problem solving). Such templates might function essentially as checklists to help students develop general approaches to dealing with different types of tasks. For example:

- ☐ I wrote down what I know from the problem.
- ☐ I understood what I had to do.
- ☐ I solved the problem.
- ☐ I wrote a concluding statement.
- ☐ I showed that I checked my work.

ASSESSMENT OF LEARNING

Assessment of learning, often called summative assessment, is less about informing teachers about what instructional decisions to take (at least at that point in time) and more about guiding decisions related to student placement or providing information to parents or the system about a student's performance. Frequently, just looking at a task does not inform the viewer about whether that task is being used formatively or summatively; many tasks work in either situation and it is simply the teacher's purpose that decides which it is.

Many considerations influence what sort of information is collected, how it is collected, when it is collected, how it is reported, and whether it is "permanent." An older, but still respected, document that informs assessment practices in mathematics in many jurisdictions is the National Council of Teachers of Mathematics Assessment Standards (National Council of Teachers of Mathematics, 1995). These standards call for assessment that reflects high-quality math, that enhances student learning, that reflects equitable practices, that is based on tasks that are open and transparent, and that supports inferences that are appropriate to the purpose.

Attention to Assessment Equity

Equity is another factor that deserves serious consideration. Equity involves not only fairness in terms of content covered. It also must be taken into account in the format of communication, in ensuring that there are no cultural biases, and in ensuring that all students get an opportunity, in whatever way works for them, to show their understanding. The differentiated assessment practices advocated here allow for accommodating a full range of student cultural as well as academic differences.

What Information Is Collected?

As discussed earlier, what teachers value informs the kinds of information they collect. The data could be focused on skills, on concepts, or on problem solving. The information could relate to content standards or to standards for mathematical practice. There is no right or wrong; it is a personal (though sometimes a group) decision.

Attention should be given to the "fairness" of the information collected in terms of how well it represents instruction (*Principles for Fair Student Assessment Practices for Education in Canada,* 1993). It is generally considered unfair to test what has not been taught. But what that means can be somewhat unclear. For some teachers, it means that the only thing they can evaluate a student on is a question that is virtually identical to one she or he has seen before; otherwise, the item seems unfair. But other teachers would argue that the only way to test, for example, problem solving is to ask a new question; otherwise, there is not really a problem. If that is the case, fairness would probably dictate that students have had problem solving experiences before, although perhaps they have not seen a problem very similar to the new one being asked about.

Should There Be Choice?

In some discipline areas, students are given choices in terms of a project, a report, or an essay for something that is considered an assessment-of-learning piece. For example, a student could show his or her learning about a particular country in whatever format he or she chooses. There could be some pieces that must be included, but there remains a lot of latitude about what the student does.

This is much less the pattern in mathematics. Here teachers, students, and parents often consider it "unfair" if students are given choice in terms of a required task. But the question remains that if the goal is for students to demonstrate their learning, does it not make sense that different students can better demonstrate their learning in different ways? In the next section, I discuss how this might suggest different formats for assessment, but the question here remains whether working with different tasks is legitimate.

For example, consider that a teacher needs to assess a 5th-grade student's ability to apply addition and subtraction of fractions using appropriate benchmarks to assess reasonableness of results and to use equations or models appropriately, as the curriculum requires.

One teacher might ask students to choose their own fractions with different denominators, create a problem that could be solved by subtracting those fractions, and solve it, also explaining how they know the answer they came up with makes sense. Another teacher might think it unfair that one student could choose 2 and 4 as denominators and another 17 and 13 and feels that the second child should get more "credit." But the teacher who gave the choice feels that the process is the same either way, so there is no need to force particular fractions.

How Data Are Collected

Most jurisdictions advocate that data be collected using a variety of methods, whether observation, conversation, a written product, or a physical performance task (Cooper, 2007). Here, too, fairness plays a role. A teacher has to decide whether it is fair that one child be allowed to respond orally when another child responds on paper. One teacher might decide that an oral response is a truer measure of what a particular student knows than a written response and will allow for this. The teacher may not do this for all students if he or she deems it is not essential for some students.

Regardless of the fairness issue, we certainly know that data gathered over time in many situations are likely to be more reliable than data gathered on one occasion in one format (Davies, 2007). For this reason alone, it is important to gather lots of data in lots of situations.

For example, a 7th-grade teacher might want to gather summative data about student understanding of formulas associated with circumference and area of a circle, as well as problem solving involving use of those formulas. He or she might collect a wide variety of data, from sources such as these:

- *Written skill questions.* For example: What is the area of this circle?

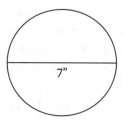

7"

- *A performance task.* For example: Show why the area of a circle is about the area of a parallelogram with a base that is about πr and a height of r (where r is the radius of the circle).
- *Oral discussion.* For example: Why would it be hard to find the area of a circle if you didn't know the formula?
- *Observation.* For example: A teacher observes whether students can apply the area of the circle formula only when given the radius, as opposed to when given the diameter or circumference instead.

Many teachers wonder whether observational data are reliable and feel the need to have something on paper to prove that their information is true. However, teachers can, for example, make a note of a date and time when they saw a certain behavior on a checklist of pertinent behaviors, can create a short note describing something observed, or can video or audio record a comment from a student. There is no reason not to trust that a teacher is being honest about data collected through observation or conversation. Parents and teachers need to realize that there is an element of subjectivity even in written work, in terms of the choice of questions used in that form of evaluation.

When Data Are Collected

Many math teachers use tests given on particular dates. But we know that students do not all work at the same pace or learn at the same pace, so the question is whether it is fair to make a final conclusion about a student's success with a particular standard based on his or her understanding on a particular date in November, for example, as opposed to at the end of the year. Most curricula are written in such a way that it is expected that students have met standards by the end of the school year.

It is more work, of course, for a teacher to go back and assess again if the need arises, but that may be what is necessary to secure valid data for assessment of learning.

How Data Are Reported

How assessment results are reported sometimes is and sometimes is not in the hands of teachers. A particular school district might, for example, require percent grades for report cards. But that should not mean to a teacher that every piece of assessment of learning needs to be recorded as a percent grade, since for many big picture skills like problem solving, there is clearly no real difference between, say, an 80% and an 85%. Teachers should record data appropriately given the nature and purpose of the task and then, if necessary, develop a conversion scheme for turning these other types of data into a format that can be factored into a numerical or other prescribed type of grade for official reporting.

Another issue is how teachers provide their evaluations to students. As mentioned earlier, there is evidence to suggest that once a teacher has put a mark on an item, students rarely, if ever, use any other provided feedback (Black & Wiliam, 2018). However, a teacher might decide to provide only comments or questions on a piece of work intended for assessment of learning, then ask students to respond to those comments, and finally, based on how students respond, assign an actual mark to the work.

For example, consider this piece of work that a teacher might assign to students:

> Lia says that when you multiply two numbers, the answer is more likely to be even than odd. Do you agree or not? Why?

A student responds:

> I don't agree because there is just as many odd numbers than even so it would be 50% of getting a odd number

This statement says something that is true (there are as many odd numbers as even ones), but it happens to incorrectly answer the question, which had to do with multiplication. The teacher could simply mark the response as 0 out of 2 or 1 out of 2 or as Level 2 or Level 1 on a rubric (depending on the criteria provided). Or the teacher could also ask the student to respond to a question like the one below before assigning a mark:

- My question asked you about multiplying two numbers. Can you show me some examples of where you multiply numbers, check whether they are even or odd, and explain how knowing that 50% of the numbers are odd means that 50% of the products are odd?

Some might see this is leading, and in some ways it is. However, if the leading is about content and the objective is to really know if students see that you only get an odd number if both numbers are odd and this happens less often than an even result, this amount of leading may yield more accurate information than the original question did.

If, however, the point of the question was to evaluate student reasoning, a practice standard, the teacher might ask a different question that is more about the reasoning itself. For example:

- You said that there are as many odds as evens and that is true. Does that mean that no matter what you do with those numbers, the results are 50%

even and 50% odd? Things you might check are: adding them, dividing them, doubling them, taking half of them, etc., and, of course, multiplying them.

Whichever path a teacher takes, the final mark should depend more, or at least as much, on how the student answers the follow-up question posed, rather than solely on the original response.

Whether Data Are Permanent

Assessment of learning generally is designed to measure student growth over time in understanding particular mathematical ideas or performing particular math skills. What do you do if a student, on a test in November, struggles with an idea, but masters the idea later? Do you continue to include the mark from the early test in the average or do you argue that all that matters is that the student knows it now, not what happened before?

I am not sure all teachers would handle the answer to this question in the same way. Although there are no rules about what to do, it would certainly be my advice to forget about that first score since it no longer reflects what the student knows, and that is all we really care about in the end.

SUMMARY

This chapter has reviewed, in a holistic way, what is involved in assessment for learning, assessment as learning, and assessment of learning.

Assessment for learning involves either diagnostic assessments or other types of formative assessments. Diagnostic assessments are designed to look at student knowledge prior to instruction to see if there are missing prerequisites or, perhaps, to see if instruction on a particular topic is even needed. Diagnostics can be based on a series of questions or perhaps a single task. Teachers must decide, in advance, what prerequisites are important enough to preassess.

Other types of formative assessment can involve formalized strategies such as exit tickets or quizzes. Or assessment information can arise informally in learning situations not explicitly designed for collecting particular data. Whatever the source, the purpose of assessment for learning is to inform teachers about whether instructional plans need to change.

Assessment as learning is useful in helping students get on or stay on a good learning path. A major consideration is ensuring that students are aware of what the teacher values in mathematical learning. Specific tools include success criteria, rubrics, analysis of samples, and self-assessment templates.

Assessment of learning involves issues of fairness, student choice, data collection methods and timing, data recording and reporting, and whether student marks should be permanent or flexible based on subsequent work.

As discussed in Chapter 1, assessment for learning, assessment of learning, and (indirectly) assessment as learning all reflect teacher beliefs about what aspects of math matter most. Chapters 4–9 will illustrate, quite specifically, what each type of assessment can look like at different grade levels and in different content domains.

• CHAPTER 3 •

Feedback

FEEDBACK is a form of communication (Higgins, Hartley, & Skelton, 2001) that in school settings generally involves a teacher's reaction—whether written, oral, or even physical—to student actions. Feedback provides an opportunity for students to reflect on their learning, based on what the teacher says or does in response.

A number of factors—including the nature of the student, the work of the student, and the learning goals the teacher has set—affect the specific type of feedback a teacher is likely to give to a student. For example, Bruno and Santos (2010) believe that feedback that might be highly useful to one student could be almost meaningless to another who does not know how to move forward with what was said. Some students respond well when someone questions what they have done, and others see a challenge as a hostile or intimidating act, so the teacher must know the personality of each individual in framing feedback.

Brookhart (2007) suggests that feedback is not useful unless students learn how to use it. Peterson and McClay (2010) go further and report on Nicol's and Macfarlane-Dick's (2006) checklist to help students better understand the kind of feedback the teacher is offering and what the various purposes of that feedback might be. In that way, Nicol and Macfarlane-Dick believe the feedback can be more useful to students. Items on their list include the following:

- Providing information about expectations (e.g., success criteria)
- Encouraging self-assessing
- Providing guidance in how to use feedback

There is a history in mathematics instruction of feedback consisting of check marks for being right or wrong, or partial versus full credit for work on a problem or a question. Until more recently, there has been less attention to feedback that is more formative or even to summative feedback that is something other than evaluative.

As discussed in the preceding chapters, it is important that teachers help students see what learning is important. This is accomplished, in part, through what is attended to in assessment, but it is also reflected in what teachers choose to comment on in feedback. That said, it is important that feedback not shut students down. Instead, it should invite them to keep reflecting. For that reason, there must be time for students to process what is communicated, and what is communicated should encourage more response from students.

This chapter explores six types of feedback, as proposed by Small and Lin (2018):

- Feedback that offers the opportunity for self-correction
- Feedback on choice of strategy
- Feedback that encourages perspective taking
- Feedback that is based on an alternative interpretation of the problem
- Feedback that encourages creativity
- Feedback that encourages extension

I also look at the immediacy of feedback and the implications of immediate versus delayed feedback, the need to give feedback on both problematic and good work, the notion of feedback as a question rather than a comment, and the need to anticipate likely errors or problems in order to plan feedback. These likely errors are often overgeneralizations, inappropriate assumptions, or other common misconceptions.

TYPES OF FEEDBACK

There is always some danger in categorizing anything, since sometimes particular situations do not fit neatly into only one category. But most feedback in math classes can be considered primarily one of the types described in the sections that follow.

I use examples from different grade levels to illustrate what the different types of feedback could look like. Note that much of the feedback is offered in the form of questions to students, not statements to them. Often a teacher's questions serve as better signals to students that they are really expected to deal with the feedback and react to it.

Feedback That Offers the Opportunity for Self-Correction

Often a student can notice his or her own error without having it pointed out. This is better for a lot of reasons. First, it avoids the sting the student might feel in being corrected. But, even more importantly, it shows the teacher that the student really does understand an idea that the teacher might have been uncertain the student understood.

For feedback that offers an opportunity for self-correction to be effective, it is important that teachers ask the sorts of questions described below regardless of whether the work is right or wrong. If a teacher gives feedback or asks questions only about wrong work, students quickly realize that a question is not really a question; it is a statement that the work is not up to par.

Here is an example of feedback that offers the opportunity for self-correction. A teacher sets a task for a 3rd-grade student:

> Draw a picture to show how to use multiplication to figure out 36 ÷ 6.

The child responds by drawing a picture that instead shows 36 ÷ 4, like this one:

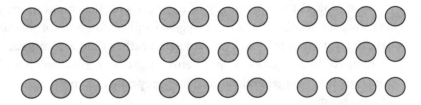

The teacher might offer feedback such as this:

• So tell me where I see the 36 in your picture. Now tell me where I see division in the picture. And where do I see the 6?

Notice that the feedback starts with two "positives": the 36 and the concept of division are correctly represented in the picture. The student then has an opportunity to see that she or he accidentally used 4 and not 6 and can fix the problem.

As noted earlier, it is critical that students who have responded correctly to a task get similar feedback, so that the feedback does not become a way of saying that the answer is incorrect.

Feedback on Choice of Strategy

Often, we encourage students to use more efficient strategies in mathematics. They might choose strategy that works, but perhaps a better strategy is available.

In giving feedback on choice of strategy, it is important to first think about the particular student and whether or not he or she is ready to try another strategy. If not, such feedback is probably not useful. But if a teacher believes that a more efficient strategy could be effectively used by the student, the teacher might give feedback to move the student in that direction.

For example, a student in 4th grade might be asked:

> Determine if the number 91 is a prime number.

To decide on a response, a student does the following:

$$91 \div 1 = 91$$
$$91 \div 2 = 45 + R1$$
$$91 \div 3 = 30 + R1$$
$$91 \div 4 = 22 + R3$$
$$91 \div 5 = 18 + R1$$
$$91 \div 6 = 15 + R1$$
$$91 \div 7 = 13$$

And she or he continues dividing 91 by *every* number up to 91.

A teacher might want students to realize, early on, that dividing by 1 is a waste of time. It never tells you whether a number is prime or not. In this case, dividing by any even number is a waste of time since 91 is odd and all multiples of evens are even. Dividing by 9 is a waste of time if dividing by 3 did not work. Dividing by 5 is a waste of time since 91 does not end in 0 or 5. Dividing by anything above 10 is a waste of time since if there were a factor above 10, there would have been one below 10.

For some students, pointing all of this out would be overwhelming. But a teacher could give feedback that deals with a little bit of this information. For example, a teacher might ask:

- I noticed that you tried dividing by 2, 4, 6, and 8. Look at your remainders each time. What do you notice? Why do you think that happened?

OR

- I noticed that when you divided 91 by 7, you got 13. What multiplication could you write? What does that tell you about other factors of 91?

Feedback That Encourages Perspective Taking

There are times in mathematical situations when students could legitimately take different perspectives on what is being asked and come up with different conclusions. Some teachers provide feedback that discourages that. They might say, for example, "*I meant . . .*" to force the student to take a perspective that was the teacher's intent. But, instead of that, a teacher might use feedback that both validates the student's decision but teaches him or her that there are alternative perspectives that could be considered too.

Here is an example from 5th grade. Students are working on classifying figures based on their properties. A teacher might set a task that asks:

> Do you think a square is more like an equilateral triangle or more like a rectangle?

The teacher might have been hoping that the student would say that the square is more like a rectangle since it is, in fact, a rectangle, but a student might choose an equilateral triangle. That also is a valid perspective. So a teacher might offer feedback like this:

- What made you think that the square was more like the equilateral triangle?

Then the teacher might also say:

- Why do you think some students would have made a different choice?

The student needs time, of course, to consider the feedback. Although it is possible a student will simply rule out the other choice, it is likely that the student will eventually realize what the teacher was hoping for—recognition that a square has all the properties of rectangles.

Feedback That Is Based on an Alternative Interpretation of the Problem

When a teacher sets a problem or task for students to work on, he or she assumes that the student is reading the problem or interpreting it the way the teacher intended. For example, a teacher might ask a 6th-grade student:

> Suppose you went to a store and bought a $49.95 item at 30% off. How much would you pay?

The student writes: $0.30 \times 49.95 = 14.985$.

There are clearly a few problems with this answer. One is that the student did not address what was paid but, instead, how much was saved. If this error becomes the focus, the teacher might use feedback that will encourage self-correction and ask, for example:

- So when a sale is 30% off, should you pay more than half or less than half of the full price?

Or, instead, a teacher might address the notion that when dealing with certain contexts, in this case money, mathematically correct answers sometimes do not make sense. The problem has to be interpreted in the right context. Here, even if the question had been about how much was saved, the student should have chosen either $14.98 or $14.99 (an argument could be made for either), but not 14.985. To get at this point, a teacher might provide feedback like this:

- So how would you show that amount with bills and coins?

Feedback That Encourages Creativity

Often some of our competent students answer our questions or problems correctly, but choose to copy procedures already established rather than branch out and devise their own way of doing things. This is very likely if they are routinely expected to copy procedures, but it is not desirable in every situation. There are many situations, not even for only strong students, where a teacher could use feedback to encourage more creativity.

For example, a 7th-grade teacher might set a task like this:

> Figure out the circumference of a circle if I tell you that the area of that circle is $5\frac{1}{2}$ square inches.

Most students dutifully figure out the radius using the formula $A = \pi r^2$. Then they figure out the diameter by doubling the radius, and then they calculate the circumference using the formula $C = \pi d$. And this is fine. But a teacher could encourage more creativity by providing feedback like this:

- Do you think you could make up a formula where you more automatically get the circumference if you know the area? (That means the circumference and area are in the same formula.)

Or a student might be asked:

> Create a problem that is solved by determining the area of a circle.

The student could come up with something pretty straightforward, like: "A circle has a radius of 2 feet. What is the area?" A teacher encouraging creativity might then ask:

- Could you make up a problem where you'd have to go through more steps to solve it?

OR

- Could you make up a problem where different students might actually get different answers?

Feedback That Encourages Extension

Trying to build creativity is a type of extension. But feedback can also be built around encouraging extensions that are less about creativity and more about just digging deeper. (I realize the difference between these two goals might be considered a fine line.)

For example, an 8th-grade teacher might set an algebra task like this one:

> Create three different systems of equations that are solved by the values $x = 4$ and $y = 5$.

A student might correctly come up with these answers:

$$2x = 8 \text{ and } 4y = 20$$
$$3x = 12 \text{ and } 8y = 40$$
$$4x = 16 \text{ and } 24y = 120$$

These are all correct and a student cannot be faulted for providing such answers. Faced with responses such as these, however, some teachers might fret that they did not put more conditions on the task. But if a teacher does put more conditions on the task, he or she is probably not sufficiently differentiating instruction for those who need a simpler task. Instead, the teacher might give feedback to students who could do more, such as this:

- Are there any equations that you could have come up with that have both x and y in the same equation?

OR

- Are there any equations that you could use where one set of equations is not just a multiple of the other set?

REACTIONS TO ALL WORK

As noted earlier, it is critical that teachers give nonevaluative feedback to both good work and problematic work. Often, teachers praise good work and ask questions about poor work. It is important to build reflection skills in students who have done good work as well. Teachers also have to make it clear that asking questions is not just a way to say that there is something wrong with the student's work.

IMMEDIACY OF FEEDBACK

There are certainly opportunities for teachers to take time to reflect on the feedback to give to students. This is particularly the case when work is submitted on paper or digitally. In this case a teacher might choose among the various types of feedback discussed earlier. It is probably overwhelming for both teacher and student to address too many points and too hard for a student to react, so being focused can help, but the area of focus must be selected by the teacher.

But often there is no opportunity for reflection or a teacher might feel it is important to give immediate feedback, most likely (though not necessarily) orally, while a student is working or just after a student has completed some or all of a task. The tricky part of this sort of feedback is that the teacher must make an almost instantaneous decision about what to focus on. This is something teachers can get better at with practice, and can get better at with anticipating and planning what is likely to happen and being ready for it.

When feedback is given while the student is still engaged in a task, it might be more meaningful to the student. Feedback during the work can help inform students as they continue the task and can lead to greater success, which is valuable too. Immediate feedback can also "nip a problem in the bud," for example, getting rid of a misunderstanding before it takes root.

The downside of immediate feedback is that a teacher needs to think fast. Particularly when working in an area of math where a teacher is less comfortable—and this is the case in many elementary schools (Karp, 1991)—it can be worrisome to the teacher to say something too quickly. However, by asking questions, rather than making statements about what is right or wrong, some of that anxiety should be alleviated.

ANTICIPATING ERRORS

Anticipating errors can make it easier for teachers to give immediate feedback. Although nobody can anticipate everything that might come up, there are some things that can be anticipated. In math, these frequently include overgeneralizations, inappropriate assumptions, and what are called common misconceptions.

Overgeneralizations

Often teachers encourage students to make generalizations from just a few examples. For example, a 3rd-grade teacher might encourage students to realize that the commutative property of multiplication (that order can be reversed when multiplying) is true based on just a few examples. So it is not surprising when students generalize from a couple of examples even when they should not.

For example, some students might be exploring prisms and note that the number of cubic units in a prism's volume is greater than the number of square units in its surface area. This does happen a lot of the time, but not always. To illuminate the error of such thinking, a teacher might set a task such as this one:

> Is it possible to create a rectangular prism where the number of square inches in the surface area is more than the number of cubic inches in its volume?

A student might immediately say "no" based on these examples:

L = 10", W = 10", H = 6"   Volume = 600 in^3 Surface Area = 440 in^2
L = 20", W = 10", H = 5"   Volume = 1000 in^3 Surface Area = 700 in^2

A teacher then might provide feedback such as this:

- I notice that you chose fairly big lengths, widths, and heights. Do you think anything would change if you used really small prisms?

Another example might be a student thinking that you always get a smaller number than you started with when you subtract. That is, of course, true for lots of numbers, but not if you subtract 0 and certainly not if you subtract a negative number. So a student might be asked to explain why 8 − (−2) = 10 and might respond that it can't be since 10 is more than 8 and you were subtracting. A teacher could just tell the student a rule: that when you subtract a negative, you increase the value of the start number. But, instead, the teacher could provide a different sort of feedback, for example:

- When you subtract a bigger number, do you usually end up with more or less than if you subtract a smaller number? So which do you think should be bigger: 8 − 0 or 8 − (−2)?

Inappropriate Assumptions

Sometimes students impose assumptions on problems that were not intended by the person who posed the problem. For example, a student might be asked to figure out the other angle in an isosceles triangle with one angle of 40°. The student might easily assume that it is the 40° angle that is duplicated, suggesting that the other angles are 40° and 100°, and not realize that the 40° angle could be the third angle in a triangle with two angles of 70°. It is a natural assumption. A teacher might offer feedback such as this:

- Which of these do you think is an isosceles triangle?

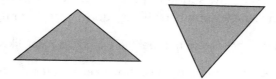

Faced with this kind of feedback, the student might realize it does not have to be the two "bottom" angles" that are the same and might self-correct.

As another example, a 5th-grade student is asked to add two fractions:

> The sum of two fractions is a fraction with a denominator of 15. What could the denominators of the two fractions that are being added be?

A student might assume, for example, that the answer would never be $\frac{10}{15}$, since $\frac{10}{15}$ would have been simplified to $\frac{2}{3}$, so that student would not see why $\frac{1}{3} + \frac{1}{3}$ could have been the original fractions. Instead the student might suggest the denominators are both 15, or one is 15 and the other is either 5 or 3, or they are 5 and 3. Feedback a teacher could offer might be:

- It does make sense to me why you chose the answers you did. What if the answer had been $\frac{15}{15}$? Are there other possibilities now?

Common Misconceptions

The term common misconceptions is often used in discussions about how students learn math, and there is a big literature on what some of these common misconceptions are (Confrey, 1990; Fazio & Siegler, 2011). Because some of these misconceptions are well known (which is why they are called common), a teacher can anticipate that they will come up and can be prepared with appropriate feedback.

One example might be that students think that when you multiply you always get a greater answer than when you add. Of course, this is not the case when you multiply by or add 0 and is not even true with examples like 7×1 compared to $7 + 1$. So, if a child suggests that this is what happens (which is, of course, also an overgeneralization), a teacher might provide feedback like this:

- Is the multiplication answer usually a lot bigger than the adding answer, or does it depend?

By helping students notice that the bigger the pair of numbers, the greater the difference between the sum and product is, students might self-correct and think about using smaller numbers. If they don't, a teacher might follow up with:

- What if the second number were a LOT smaller, like 0 or 1?

Another common misconception is encountered when students use fractions. Many students believe that if a fraction has a greater numerator and a greater denominator, it must be a greater fraction. For example, $4 > 2$ and $5 > 3$ so they might conclude that $\frac{4}{5} > \frac{2}{3}$. This, too, is an overgeneralization. Again, feedback is needed to lead students to a better conclusion. A teacher might say:

- I notice that you chose fractions where the numerators and denominators are 1 apart. What if they were both 2 apart? 10 apart? What if they were different distances apart?

Hopefully students will self-correct and realize that, for example, $\frac{7}{100} < \frac{6}{5}$ and not the reverse.

SUMMARY

This chapter has focused on the important role of feedback in furthering the learning of students. Feedback is, by its nature, communication with students, so it is important that teachers think about what they wish to communicate and how to transmit that information in a way that encourages students to reflect productively on their learning.

It is important that feedback be given to all students, for good work and for poor work, and that feedback leads to reflection and metacognition, rather than simply evaluates the quality of work. Six different types of feedback can accomplish these goals:

- Feedback that offers the opportunity for self-correction
- Feedback on choice of strategy
- Feedback that encourages perspective taking
- Feedback that is based on an alternative interpretation of the problem
- Feedback that encourages creativity
- Feedback that encourages extension

Providing immediate feedback presents challenges for the teacher but yields advantages for the student. The challenges can be lessened to a degree by anticipating what students might do—particularly engaging in overgeneralizations, inappropriate assumptions, and common misconceptions—and planning ahead for probing or scaffolding responses.

BEGINNING with the next chapter, the discussion shifts from the theoretical to the practical. Chapters 4–9 flesh out quite fully what assessment and feedback could look like at a particular grade level in a particular content domain. Each of the six chapters will emphasize a standard for mathematical practice as well.

Although the discussions in the remaining chapters begin with a statement of commonly used standards for illustrative purposes, the math content and practices discussed here translate easily to curricula based on different sets of standards. And while details of the content pertain to particular grade levels, many of the ideas presented can be adapted to other grade levels.

CHAPTER 4

Operations and Algebraic Thinking, Grade 3

Assessment and Feedback

THIS CHAPTER explores assessment and feedback in the area of operations and algebraic thinking for students in Grade 3. The discussion also highlights a mathematical practice standard focused on reasoning abstractly and quantitatively. While the standards illustrated here apply to the Grade 3 level, other standards schemes might assign some of these concepts and skills to learners one grade higher or lower. Teachers should tailor the information provided to their particular situation.

THE MATH THAT MATTERS

Representative curriculum standards in the content domain of operations and algebraic thinking at the 3rd-grade level can be expressed as follows:

Operations and Algebraic Thinking
Represent and solve problems involving multiplication and division.

1. Interpret products of whole numbers, e.g., interpret 5 × 7 as the total number of objects in 5 groups of 7 objects each. *For example, describe a context in which a total number of objects can be expressed as 5 × 7.*
2. Interpret whole-number quotients of whole numbers, e.g., interpret 56 ÷ 8 as the number of objects in each share when 56 objects are partitioned equally into 8 shares, or as a number of shares when 56 objects are partitioned into equal shares of 8 objects each. *For example, describe a context in which a number of shares or a number of groups can be expressed as 56 ÷ 8.*
3. Use multiplication and division within 100 to solve word problems in situations involving equal groups, arrays, and measurement quantities, e.g., by using drawings and equations with a symbol for the unknown number to represent the problem.
4. Determine the unknown whole number in a multiplication or division equation relating three whole numbers. For example, determine the unknown number

that makes the equation true in each of the equations 8 × ? = 48, 5 = □ ÷ 3, 6 × 6 = ?

Understand properties of multiplication and the relationship between multiplication and division.

5. Apply properties of operations as strategies to multiply and divide. *Examples: If 6 × 4 = 24 is known, then 4 × 6 = 24 is also known. (Commutative property of multiplication.) 3 × 5 × 2 can be found by 3 × 5 = 15, then 15 × 2 = 30, or by 5 × 2 = 10, then 3 × 10 = 30. (Associative property of multiplication.) Knowing that 8 × 5 = 40 and 8 × 2 = 16, one can find 8 × 7 as 8 × (5 + 2) = (8 × 5) + (8 × 2) = 40 + 16 = 56. (Distributive property.)*

6. Understand division as an unknown-factor problem. *For example, find 32 ÷ 8 by finding the number that makes 32 when multiplied by 8.*

Multiply and divide within 100.

7. Fluently multiply and divide within 100, using strategies such as the relationship between multiplication and division (e.g., knowing that 8 × 5 = 40, one knows 40 ÷ 5 = 8) or properties of operations. By the end of Grade 3, know from memory all products of two one-digit numbers.

Solve problems involving the four operations, and identify and explain patterns in arithmetic.

8. Solve two-step word problems using the four operations. Represent these problems using equations with a letter standing for the unknown quantity. Assess the reasonableness of answers using mental computation and estimation strategies including rounding.

9. Identify arithmetic patterns (including patterns in the addition table or multiplication table), and explain them using properties of operations. *For example, observe that 4 times a number is always even, and explain why 4 times a number can be decomposed into two equal addends.*

(CCSSI, 2010)

Although there is some attention to patterns in Standard 9 above and to problems involving addition and subtraction in Standard 8, the primary focus in this domain at the 3rd-grade level is clearly on developing a solid grounding in multiplication and division, on when multiplication and division are used (i.e., in which situations), and on properties and strategies for calculating small products and quotients. Thus, the majority of the suggested tools for assessment and items for feedback in this chapter focus on multiplication and division and Standards 1–7 in the list above.

Tasks and questions in this chapter draw attention to a mathematical practice standard for reasoning abstractly and quantitatively. A common expression of such a standard is the following:

Reason abstractly and quantitatively.

Mathematically proficient students make sense of quantities and their relationships in problem situations. They bring two complementary abilities to bear on problems involving quantitative relationships: the ability to decontextualize—to abstract a given situation and represent it symbolically and manipulate the representing symbols as if they have a life of their own, without necessarily attending to their referents—and the ability to contextualize, to pause as needed during the manipulation process in order to probe into the referents for the symbols involved. Quantitative reasoning entails habits of creating a coherent representation of the problem at hand; considering the units involved; attending to the meaning of quantities, not just how to compute them; and knowing and flexibly using different properties of operations and objects.   (CCSSI, 2010)

Meanings of the Operations

Multiplication

What should students understand about what multiplication and division mean? To a student, a multiplication like 4 × 3 should mean:

- The total if there are 4 groups of 3
- The area, in square units, of a rectangle that has a length of 4 and width of 3
- 3 + 3 + 3 + 3

These meanings might be modeled in many ways, such as equal sets of counters that are not formed in arrays, arrays, rectangles made of square tiles, or jumps on a number line. For example:

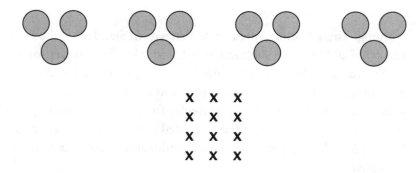

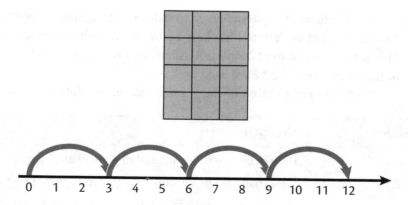

Each of the different pictures or meanings of multiplication is equivalent to each of the others. For example, looking at the model for area of a rectangle, you can see 3 + 3 + 3 + 3 by counting one row at a time, you can see 4 groups of 3 by looking at one row at a time, and you can see an array by thinking of each square as the equivalent of one **x** in the array.

Division

Division can be thought of as either determining the size of a single group if the total and the number of equal groups are known, or determining the number of groups if the total and the size of the equal groups are known.

In each picture for multiplication above, there are 12 items split up into 4 groups, and each group has a size of 3; therefore, each diagram shows 12 ÷ 4. A division is implicit in each of the multiplication situations; you can't see a multiplication without also seeing a division.

But sometimes 12 ÷ 4 means that you want to know how many groups of 4 there are in a set of size 12. You can see that in the array, if you count each column as a group, or in the rectangle, if you count each column as a group. You can readily see 4 + 4 + 4 if you look at either the array or the rectangle, but it is less clear in the picture of 4 groups of 3 circles, even though, of course, there are 12 items there also.

Division can also be thought of as repeated subtraction. For example, 12 ÷ 4 could be interpreted as asking how many 4s can be subtracted from 12 to get to 0. This might be modeled on a number line:

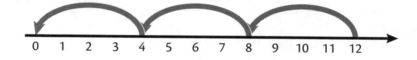

It is important that students see why determining how many groups of 4 are in 12 is equivalent to determining how many are in each of 4 groups making up 12. This is because sharing 12 among 4 usually involves creating sets of 4 (one for each of the shares) until all 12 are used up.

Students need to think of each of the equations below as indicated:

Equation	Situation
$3 \times 5 = n$	How many are there altogether if there are 3 groups of 5?
$3 \times n = 15$	How many are in a group if 3 equal groups make a total of 15?
$n \times 5 = 15$	How many groups of 5 are there if there are 15 items?
$24 \div 3 = n$	How many are there in each group if 3 equal groups make 24?
$24 \div n = 8$	How many groups of size 8 are there in 24?
$n \div 3 = 8$	How many items are there if you can make 3 equal groups of 8?

Properties and Principles

Students need to understand properties and principles related to multiplication and division and be able to use the ideas to solve problems. Students should not only know the properties; they should know why they make sense.

A few of the important properties and principles are described below:

Property or principle	Essence of the property or principle
The commutative property of multiplication: $a \times b = b \times a$	Notice that the commutative property also explains why, if $c \div a = b$, then $c \div b = a$. For example, since $3 \times 4 = 12$ and so does $4 \times 3 = 12$, $12 \div 3 = 4$ and $12 \div 4 = 3$.
	A good way to see this property is by looking at the rectangle or array model.
The associative property of multiplication: $a \times (b \times c) = (a \times b) \times c$	Another way to think of this property is that you can multiply in parts. For example, since $2 \times 4 = 8$, to multiply by 8 you can multiply first by 4 and then by 2. So, for instance, $8 \times 7 = (2 \times 4) \times 7 = 2 \times (4 \times 7)$.

The associative property of multiplication (*continued*)	The associative property also helps explain why you can multiply both the dividend and divisor by the same amount without changing the quotient. For example: If $(3 \times 4) \div (3 \times 2) = k$, that is because $(3 \times 2) \times k = 3 \times 4$. But $(3 \times 2) \times k = 3 \times (2 \times k)$ because of the associative property. So, if $3 \times (2 \times k) = 3 \times 4$, then $2 \times k = 4$ and $k = 4 \div 2$.
	A more everyday way to look at this is that if you have 3 times as much stuff to share among 3 times as many people, they would each get the same amount as if you had just shared the original stuff among the original number of people.
The distributive property of multiplication over addition (or subtraction): $a \times (b + c) = (a \times b) + (a \times c)$ OR $a \times (b - c) = (a \times b) - (a \times c)$	The distributive property allows us to figure out, for example, the number in 9 groups of 4 (or 9×4) by figuring out the number in 5 groups of 4 and then adding the number in 4 more groups of 4. It is a very useful strategy for building answers to larger number products by using smaller products to get there.
The zero property: $a \times 0 = 0 \times a = 0$	This is a quick way to say that if you have a lot of nothing, you have nothing, or if you have no groups of anything, you don't have anything.
The one property: $a \times 1 = 1 \times a = a$	This is a quick way to say that if you have one group of something, you have just that something, or if you have a bunch of groups of 1, the total number you have is the number of groups.

ASSESSMENT FOR LEARNING AND FEEDBACK

In planning and conducting assessment for learning and feedback, a teacher should be guided by applicable standards. For 3rd-grade work in operations and algebraic thinking, significant topics have been highlighted in the preceding pages.

To begin, a teacher might decide to administer one or more diagnostic tasks or questions to determine students' readiness for the work to come. As learning proceeds, a variety of formative assessments, both informal and more structured, along with probing or scaffolding feedback, can help keep students on track to meeting standards.

Here I provide numerous sample tasks and questions, with suggested feedback, as well as an observation checklist (p. 57) specific to topics covered in this chapter.

Diagnostic Task

> - Take 24 square tiles. Choose a number of children to share them. How many tiles would each child get? Write what you did using math symbols.
> - Repeat with a different number of children.
> - Now take a different number of tiles and repeat the task.

With this task, you can learn whether students can physically perform divisions (which implicitly involve multiplications). You can see whether they recognize what numbers work nicely for sharing versus ones that do not. You can also learn whether they already know about multiplication and division symbols or still use repeated addition or repeated subtraction. This is information you can use in moving the students forward.

Diagnostic Questions

> Use models or draw a picture to show each of these expressions. Then tell how much each is worth.
>
> $$4 + 4 + 4$$
> $$12 - 3 - 3 - 3 - 3$$
> $$2 \times 5$$
> $$12 \div 4$$

If you learn, through the task or the questions, that students are simply not ready to think about equal groups yet, you have to make a decision about what kind of additional work might be needed before moving on to the standards you want to address.

Tasks Designed for Formative Assessment

What follows is a sampling of tasks that might be used for formative assessment of 3rd-grade students working in operations and algebraic thinking. The discussion of each task includes a set of suggested success criteria that might be developed with students. For some tasks, examples of student work are shown, along with suggested feedback. For other tasks, I offer comments about stumbling blocks students might encounter and suggestions for how to follow up to help them overcome obstacles and increase the depth of their understanding.

Task 1

> Choose a bunch of numbers. Multiply each one by 5. What do you notice? Why does that happen?

Success Criteria

☐ I choose at least a few numbers and multiply them by 5.
☐ I look at the products and say some things that are true about all of them.
☐ I tell why I think those things turned out to be true.

Student Sample with Feedback

This student's response shows that some good things are happening. She is clearly suggesting that "fives numbers" are numbers you say when you count by 5, but she doesn't express it that way. As well, she does not explain why this is what should happen. Feedback might involve questions like these:

- What did you mean by "fives numbers"?
- Are you sure you would keep getting fives numbers if you used higher numbers for the first number?
- Why do you think you do get fives numbers?

Task 2

> Continue this story to make it a division problem.
>
> Erica had 36 cookies.

Success Criteria

☐ I add some words and a question to the first sentence to make a division problem.

☐ I tell how I know it is a division problem.

Student Sample with Feedback

She wants to share them with her friend.

$36 \div 2 =$

Many teachers might be disappointed that the student did not actually solve the problem or explain why this is a division problem, but, in truth, neither is required as the task is stated, even though the latter is mentioned in the success criteria. You might acknowledge that you are quite happy with the response but are still wondering about a few things, for example:

- Are all division problems sharing problems or only some of them?
- Are all sharing problems division problems or only some of them?

Another Student Sample with Feedback

The student below gave quite a different response:

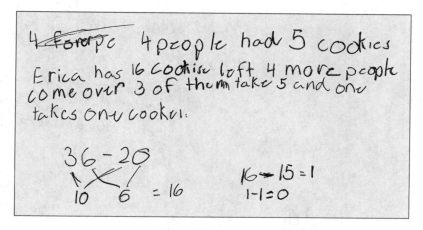

This response is very complex. There is implicit multiplication in the problem (e.g., 4×5 and 3×5) and subtraction is clearly suggested, but the division is somewhat hidden. In fact, the student has really shown that $36 = (7 \times 5) + 1$, since 7 people each took 5 cookies and 1 cookie was left.

Some teachers would be delighted with a response like the one above, assuming that the student knew why this was a division question. However, other teachers might worry about whether the student really did know why this was a division. Either way, you might ask:

- How would you explain to someone who did not know why this was a division problem why it is one? What was actually divided by what?
- Is it still a division problem if there is a remainder?

Task 3

> Which of these questions does knowing $4 \times 10 = 40$ help you with? How?
>
> 4×5 8×10 4×11

Success Criteria

- ☐ I tell whether I could figure out each multiplication by knowing that $4 \times 10 = 40$.
- ☐ If not, I tell why not.
- ☐ If I could figure out the multiplication, I explain how and why it works.

Student Sample with Feedback

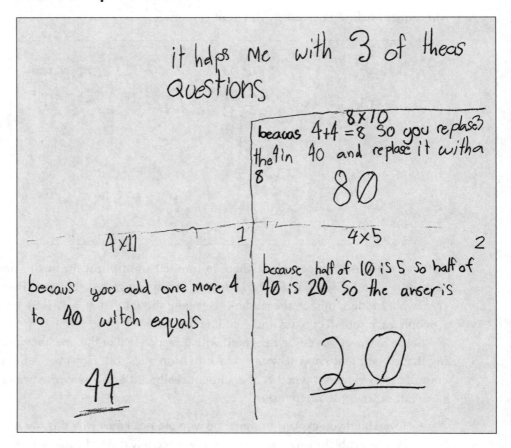

The response provided gives you a lot of information about this student's thinking. But you might have some worries when the student talks about replacing the 4 in 40 with an 8. So you might ask:

- If I had asked how knowing 4 × 9 = 36 would help with 8 × 9 = 72, there would have been no 4 in the result to replace. What would you do then?

You might also ask:

- Why did you add one more 4 to 40 for 4 × 11?

Task 4

> Think about the following two problems:
>
> 1. Which of the two problems below could you solve by multiplying? How do you know? Write the equation and solve that problem. Rewrite the other problem so that it becomes a multiplication problem. Then write the equation and solve it.
>
>   a. Kenji bought a game for $3 and a toy for $4 at a yard sale. How much did he spend altogether?
>
>   b. Pena bought 3 toys for $4 each at the yard sale. How much did she spend altogether?
>
> 2. Now do the same with the four parts below. If it's a multiplication problem, write the equation and solve it. If it's not, change it so it is. Then write the equation and solve it.
>
>   a. There were 18 toys for sale. Someone bought 6 of them. How many are left?
>
>   b. Connor bought 8 games for $3 each. How much did he spend?
>
>   c. Ari bought 5 toys, then another 5, and then another 5. How many did he buy?
>
>   d. Kelly divided 32 toys equally among 4 tables. How many toys were on each table?
>
> (Adapted from Small, 2018)

Success Criteria

☐ I change problems that cannot be solved by multiplying so they become multiplication problems.

☐ I write multiplication equations for each multiplication problem.

☐ I explain what makes a problem a multiplication one.

Suggestions About What to Look For and How to Follow Up

Many students will incorrectly identify a problem as a multiplication one if it has the "right numbers" in it. For example, Question 2a might be called multiplication since students might associate 18 and 6 with multiplication. You might ask:

• Suppose the words were the same but the numbers changed to 14 and 6. Would it still be a multiplication?

Some students will not recognize that any division question (e.g., 2d) can also be viewed as a multiplication. This needs to come out, so you might ask:

- I see why you thought it was a division. But Kelly thought it was a multiplication. Could she be right too?

Some students will not realize that a question like 2c could be thought of as either an addition or a multiplication. Depending on which the student initially chooses, you might ask:

- Is there another operation you could have used to solve it instead?

It is vital to ask questions like the ones listed below and elicit student reaction:

- What helped you recognize a multiplication problem?
- Some people might see a problem as a multiplication and some might see it as not a multiplication. Why might both sides be right?
- What do you do to create a multiplication problem?

Task 5

> Jennifer had to use exactly 40 pick-up sticks to build a bunch of identical shapes.
>
> - How many shapes could she make and what kind of shape would they be?
> - Think of different possibilities.
> - Do you think there are other answers?

Ideally, students will decontextualize this problem, realizing that they are looking for pairs of numbers to multiply to get 40, for example, 10 shapes each with 4 sides since $4 \times 10 = 40$, or 8 shapes with 5 sides each, and so on.

Success Criteria

☐ I think about what kinds of shapes they could be if they were all the same and how many I could make.

☐ I figure out if I have thought of all of the possibilities.

Suggestions About What to Look For and How to Follow Up

Many students will not even know where to begin, so clearly it could be helpful to supply 40 pick-up sticks or 40 pencils or 40 toothpicks. Then you might ask questions like these:

- Could you make shapes with 4 sides? What would they look like? How many could you make?
- Could you make shapes with 3 sides? What would they look like? How many could you make? Would that use all of the sticks?
- Could you make shapes with 20 sides? Why or why not?

A student might wonder if a shape could have sides made up of more than one pick-up stick. It is important that the teacher allow the student to make the decision and investigate. For example, a student might end up with 5 shapes like this:

Another student might wonder if the pick-up sticks are all the same size. Feedback could be:

- Why don't you decide if it makes a difference?

ASSESSMENT AS LEARNING

By learning to self-assess, students can more easily measure their own understanding and make adjustments in their work if necessary. They can gain this important skill by practicing regularly, with peer and teacher support, and using techniques (described in Chapter 2) such as success criteria, rubrics, samples, and self-assessment templates.

In this focus on operations and algebraic thinking, success criteria attached to particular tasks described in the preceding section would be particularly relevant.

ASSESSMENT OF LEARNING

Assessment of learning begins with a teacher's decision about which ideas, skills, and mathematical practices are important and should be monitored, depending on curriculum standards that need to be met. The assessment tools that follow address the content standards and mathematical practice standard described at the beginning of this chapter.

Examples of skill questions, concept questions, a performance task (with rubric), and an observation checklist are provided. For each of these forms of assessment, there are, of course, many possible choices; here I provide simply a sampling of appropriate options. A teacher might use some, but not all, of these tools or individual items. Which are used depends on whether observations have left the teacher unsure about student skills or understandings in particular areas.

Skill Questions

1. You multiply □ × □ (two numbers under 10). The answer is between 20 and 40. What could you have multiplied? List as many possibilities as you can.

2. How much more is:
   a. 5×3 than 5×1?
   b. 4×7 than 4×5?
   c. 3×8 than 2×8?

3. What number is missing if:
   a. 7×8 is 21 more than □ × 5?
   b. 7×6 is 3 less than □ × 5?
   c. 7×3 is 9 less than □ × 5?

4. Calculate each of these:
   a. 4×5
   b. 2×8
   c. 3×9

   [*You might add more fact questions for multiplication, if you wish, perhaps a total of five small facts (both numbers under 5) and five larger ones (numbers from 6 to 9 as at least one factor).*]

5. Calculate each of these:
   a. $35 \div 5$
   b. $9 \div 3$
   c. $56 \div 8$

   [*You might add more fact questions for division, if you wish, some involving divisors under 6 and some 6 or more.*]

Concept Questions

1. Write problems that include 4 and 5 and that fit the rules below:
   a. One that could be solved by knowing that $4 \times 5 = 20$
   b. One that could NOT be solved by knowing that $4 \times 5 = 20$
2. Write problems that include 35 and 7 and that fit the rules below:
   a. One that could be solved by knowing that $35 \div 7 = 5$
   b. One that could NOT be solved by knowing that $35 \div 7 = 5$
3. Show two different models for what each means:
   a. 4×6
   b. $30 \div 6$
4. What is different, or is anything different, about the role of the number 5 in these two equations?
   a. $\square \div 4 = 5$
   b. $5 \times \square = 35$
5. How are the two following problems related? Explain.
   Problem A: There were 8 students who each put in $4 to buy their coach a gift. How much did they collect altogether?
   Problem B: Mom made 32 cookies. She divided them up onto 4 plates. How many cookies were on each plate?
6. Explain how and why each of these strategies works.
   a. Using 7×2 to figure out 7×4
   b. Using 4×8 and 2×8 to figure out 6×8
   c. Using $12 \div 3$ to figure out $24 \div 6$
7. What (other) single-digit multiplication facts could help you figure out each of these and how?
   a. 8×6
   b. 5×4
   c. $24 \div 4$
   d. $42 \div 7$
8. Solve each of these problems. Show your thinking in working through each one using pictures or words or both.
   a. One notebook costs $3. How much would 6 of them cost?
   b. There are 6 markers in each box. I bought 48 markers. How many boxes did I buy?
   c. I have to divide up 18 library books into 6 equal piles for the 6 groups in the class. How many books go on each pile?

Note that a number of these questions deal with the mathematical practice standard related to reasoning abstractly and quantitatively. In several cases, students take a mathematical situation and create a contextual one; in other cases, students are asked to mathematize a contextual situation.

The only thing really missing in terms of this practice standard is asking students to decontextualize a contextual situation, play with the math, and then apply the work back to the context. This might be brought out by asking a question like this one:

> - Solve this problem: Abigail had 9 nickels. How much was it worth, in cents?
> - Create another calculation that you know has double the answer.
> - Change the original problem as little as possible so that the doubled answer would be the correct answer.

Performance Task

> Create a game using dice that could help you practice multiplication and division facts. Tell what the rules are. Make sure your game works.

A rubric, such as the one shown here, might be used to evaluate a student's success with this performance task:

	Level 1	Level 2	Level 3	Level 4
Criteria	The student	The student	The student	The student
Creating an appropriate game	• creates a game that provides little or no practice with multiplication or division facts	• creates a game that provides some practice with limited multiplication or division facts	• creates a game that provides significant practice with multiplication facts (to 9 × 9) or division facts (from 81 ÷ 9)	• creates a unique game that provides practice with multiplication and division facts and ensures a wide range of facts (to 9 × 9 and from 81 ÷ 9) is practiced

Writing game rules	• includes unclear rules	• includes somewhat clear rules	• includes clear rules	• includes very clear rules, provides an example to illustrate the rules, and/or provides rule variations
Testing the game	• does not test the rules of the game	• tests the rules of the game but does not modify the game as a result	• tests the rules of the game, modifying as needed	• tests the rules of the game in a systematic way and revises to improve the game

(Adapted from Small, 2018)

Observation Checklist

As teachers observe students throughout their work on this topic, they should take particular note of whether students:

☐ show an awareness of different meanings of multiplication and division
☐ use different and appropriate models to represent multiplication or division situations
☐ use the relationship between multiplication and division to help them divide
☐ use a simple fact to help them correctly calculate a more complex one

Putting It Together

Teachers also have to decide how to weight the various pieces of evidence they have gathered. There is no firm and fast rule, but for a topic that focuses on skills to the extent found in standards in this area, but also with a significant conceptual component, I suggest that weights might be something like this:

Observations	70%	(Observation of both skill and concept work, with a heavier emphasis on concepts.)
Skills	10%	(Additional skill items asked at the conclusion of the topic.)
Concepts	10%	(Additional concept items asked at the conclusion of the topic.)
Performance Task	10%	(Performed at the conclusion of the topic.)

Observations are given the highest weight because they are more frequent and probably more reliable than the other forms of assessment. Note that concepts are rated as more critical than skills because there is a lot of attention to concepts in standards in this topic.

SUMMARY

This chapter has modeled what assessment for learning, assessment as learning, and assessment of learning could look like in teaching 3rd-grade students the content needed to meet standards related to operations and algebraic thinking. The illustrated assessments have also highlighted a mathematical practice standard for reasoning abstractly and quantitatively.

At this level, work in operations and algebraic thinking focuses on multiplication and division and their meanings and uses.

The chapter features numerous samples of questions and tasks that can be used to elicit diagnostic, formative, and summative data; suggestions on what to observe as students work; and illustrations of feedback a teacher might give. Finally, a suggested weighting scheme is provided for evaluating the array of assessment evidence that can be collected.

• CHAPTER 5 •

Number and Operations in Base Ten, Grade 4
Assessment and Feedback

THIS CHAPTER explores assessment and feedback in the area of number and operations in base ten for students in Grade 4. The discussion also highlights a mathematical practice standard focused on looking for and making use of structure. While the standards illustrated here apply to the Grade 4 level, other standards schemes might assign some of these concepts and skills to learners one grade higher or lower. Teachers should tailor the information provided to their particular situation.

THE MATH THAT MATTERS

Representative curriculum standards in the content domain of number and operations in base ten at the 4th-grade level can be expressed as follows:

Number and Operations in Base Ten
Generalize place value understanding for multi-digit whole numbers.

1. Recognize that in a multi-digit whole number, a digit in one place represents ten times what it represents in the place to its right. *For example, recognize that 700 ÷ 70 = 10 by applying concepts of place value and division.*
2. Read and write multi-digit whole numbers using base-ten numerals, number names, and expanded form. Compare two multi-digit numbers based on meanings of the digits in each place, using >, =, and < symbols to record the results of comparisons.
3. Use place value understanding to round multi-digit whole numbers to any place.

Use place value understanding and properties of operations to perform multi-digit arithmetic.

4. Fluently add and subtract multi-digit whole numbers using the standard algorithm.

5. Multiply a whole number of up to four digits by a one-digit whole number, and multiply two two-digit numbers, using strategies based on place value and the properties of operations. Illustrate and explain the calculation by using equations, rectangular arrays, and/or area models.

6. Find whole-number quotients and remainders with up to four-digit dividends and one-digit divisors, using strategies based on place value, the properties of operations, and/or the relationship between multiplication and division. Illustrate and explain the calculation by using equations, rectangular arrays, and/or area models.

(CCSSI, 2010)

A number of different topics are involved in this strand: place value concepts, concepts related to addition and subtraction of large numbers, and concepts related to multiplication and division involving large numbers.

Tasks and questions in this chapter draw attention to a mathematical practice standard of looking for and making use of structure. A common expression of such a standard is the following:

Look for and make use of structure.

Mathematically proficient students look closely to discern a pattern or structure. Young students, for example, might notice that three and seven more is the same amount as seven and three more, or they may sort a collection of shapes according to how many sides the shapes have. Later, students will see 7×8 equals the well remembered $7 \times 5 + 7 \times 3$, in preparation for learning about the distributive property. In the expression $x^2 + 9x + 14$, older students can see the 14 as 2×7 and the 9 as $2 + 7$. They recognize the significance of an existing line in a geometric figure and can use the strategy of drawing an auxiliary line for solving problems. They also can step back for an overview and shift perspective. They can see complicated things, such as some algebraic expressions, as single objects or as being composed of several objects. For example, they can see $5 - 3(x - y)^2$ as 5 minus a positive number times a square and use that to realize that its value cannot be more than 5 for any real numbers x and y.

(CCSSI, 2010)

Place Value

What do we want students to understand about place value concepts in Grade 4?

The idea	An elaboration
A digit's value changes depending on its placement in a number.	A digit in one position of a number is worth a different value than the same digit in another position. In particular, the value is multiplied by 10 for each move to the left or divided by 10 for each move to the right. For example, one of the 5s in 5452 is worth 100 times as much as the other 5.
Only 10 digits are needed.	Some teachers might want students to understand the "efficiency" of our place value system, which allows us to use just 10 digits to describe an infinite number of numbers.
Numbers can be written in expanded form, not just standard form.	Although we usually write large numbers using digits (e.g., 40,234), it is also possible to write a number in what is called expanded form (e.g., either as 4 ten thousands + 2 hundreds + 3 tens + 4 ones, or as 40,000 + 200 + 30 + 4).
	The expanded form is designed to make it easier to read the number, write the number, model the number, and make sense of how it compares to other numbers.
	Students might recognize that in the expanded form, you write one addend for each non-zero digit, so large numbers or small numbers might have the same number of terms in their expanded notation, depending on how many non-zero digits they include.
Comparing numbers is easier with a place value system.	Another feature of the place value system is that it makes it relatively easy to know which of two whole numbers is more or less than another.
	Students need to make sense of how the place value system does this, on the surface level in counting numbers of digits, but really through estimation. For example, 42,156 > 3457 since it has more digits, but really it is greater because "about 40 thousand" is more than "about 3 thousand."

Rounding is a way to estimate.	To get a sense of the size of a number, students might estimate by using rounding. Students should not only learn the rounding rules but should also understand why rounding is one form, but not the only form, of estimation and why we might make different decisions about how to round a number, depending on the context.

Adding and Subtracting Multi-Digit Numbers

The focus at this grade level is on adding and subtracting whole numbers using the standard algorithms. Although students should be able to execute the algorithms, it is equally important that they can explain why the steps make sense and that they can tell whether or not their answer is reasonable and why. In terms of the steps, students should have an understanding of the usefulness of decomposing numbers into multiples of powers of ten (i.e., tens, hundreds, thousands, etc.) to make addition and subtraction easier and they must understand why we regroup the way we do in performing each standard algorithm.

Students also need to know when to add and subtract, but this knowledge falls more under the content domain of operations and algebraic thinking (see Chapter 4) than under number and operations.

Multiplying and Dividing Multi-Digit Numbers

When multiplying and dividing multi-digit numbers by single-digit numbers, or 2-digit numbers by 2-digit numbers, students need to make sense of models that help explain the process as well as make sense of the role of the distributive property in those operations.

For example, 5 × 2314 could be modeled in either of these ways:

	2000	300	10	4
5	10,000	1500	50	20

_OR_

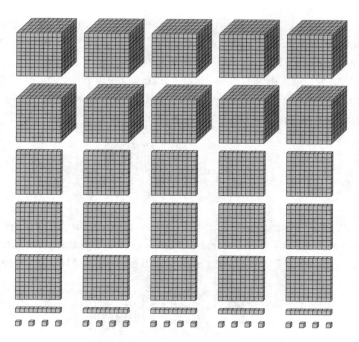

In each case, the student sees that $5 \times 2314 = 5 \times 2000 + 5 \times 300 + 5 \times 10 + 5 \times 4 = 10,000 + 1500 + 50 + 20 = 11,570$. Note that a rectangular model is used in each case to emphasize how a product can be thought of as the area of a rectangle with a given length and width.

Similarly, a 2-digit by 2-digit multiplication can be modeled and thought of in terms of a rectangular area, using the distributive property. For example, 22×31 might be modeled in either of these ways:

	30	1
20	600	20
2	60	2

OR

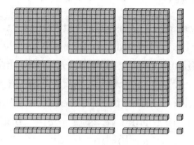

In either case, 22×31 is displayed as $600 + 20 + 60 + 2 = 682$.

Again, it is important that students have a sense of the size of the answer; for example, 5 × 2314 might be estimated by 5 × 2000 = 10,000, and 22 × 31 can be thought of as a bit more than 20 × 30 = 600.

Modeling a division of 2050 ÷ 5 requires application of the distributive property. The student begins by showing 2050 and then rearranges the amount into 5 equal shares and reports the size of each share.

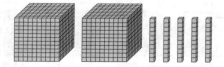

With a "typical" 2050 model (shown above), the student realizes that she or he cannot share the 2 thousand cubes to create 5 equal piles and thus trades the 2 large cubes for 20 hundred flats. Now 5 groups of 410 can be formed.

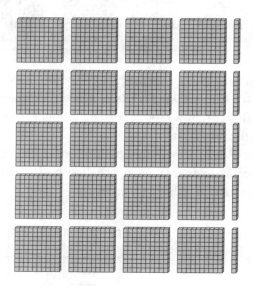

ASSESSMENT FOR LEARNING AND FEEDBACK

In planning and conducting assessment for learning and feedback, a teacher should be guided by applicable standards. For 4th-grade work in number and operations in base ten, significant topics have been highlighted in the preceding pages.

To begin, a teacher might decide to administer one or more diagnostic tasks or questions to determine students' readiness for the work to come. As learning proceeds, a variety of formative assessments, both informal and more structured, along with probing or scaffolding feedback, can help keep students on track to meeting curriculum goals.

Here I provide numerous sample tasks and questions, with suggested feedback, as well as an observation checklist (p. 77) specific to topics covered in this chapter.

Diagnostic Task

> 1. You need to figure out 4×23.
>   a. If you were drawing or modeling 4×23 without counting out lots of items, what would the picture or model look like?
>   b. How would your picture or model help you figure out the answer?
>   c. What simpler multiplication might help you figure out 4×23 without a model? How?
> 2. You need to figure out $92 \div 4$.
>   a. If you were drawing or modeling $92 \div 4$ without counting out lots of items, what would the picture or model look like?
>   b. How would your picture or model help you figure out the answer?
>   c. What simpler division might help you figure out $92 \div 4$ without a model? How?

With this task, you can learn whether students recognize how to model multiplications and divisions without counting by ones, since the task asked them to not use lots of items. You might also see how students relate more complex questions to simpler ones.

Alternatively, as illustrated below, you might use similar operations (4×23 and $92 \div 4$) but pose questions that are somewhat more leading, for example, telling students what model to use and requiring the use of decomposition.

Diagnostic Questions

> 1. Use base ten blocks to show 4×23.
> 2. What are four or five different ways you can fill this in?
> $$4 \times 23 = 4 \times \underline{\quad} + 4 \times \underline{\quad}$$
> 3. Use base ten blocks to show $92 \div 4$.
> 4. What are four or five different ways you can fill this in?
> $$92 \div 4 = \underline{\quad} \div 4 + \underline{\quad} \div 4$$

If you learn, through the task or the questions, that students are simply not ready to think about the distributive property or rectangular models for larger computations, you have to make a decision about what kind of additional work might be needed before moving on to the standards you want to address.

Tasks Designed for Formative Assessment

The tasks described here are a sampling of tasks that might be used for formative assessment of 4th-grade students working in number and operations in base ten. The discussion of each task includes a set of suggested success criteria that might be developed with students. For some tasks, examples of student work are shown, along with suggested feedback. For other tasks, I offer comments about stumbling blocks students might encounter and suggestions for how to follow up to help them overcome obstacles and increase the depth of their understanding.

Task 1

> - Choose several 3-digit numbers.
> - Write each in expanded form.
> - Show how writing the numbers in expanded form could help you multiply each by 4.
> - Figure out the product for each of the numbers by using what you just did.

Ideally, students will realize that they can multiply each part of the expanded form by 4 and add the results.

Success Criteria

☐ I choose at least a few 3-digit numbers.
☐ I write each in expanded form.
☐ I use a model or picture or words or a combination to show how the expanded form helps me multiply my number by 4.

Suggestions About What to Look For and How to Follow Up

Students need to realize that no matter what computation you do, when one or both of the numbers are fairly large, it is helpful to decompose the large number(s) into pieces and simplify the problem by applying properties of the operations and appropriately combining the resulting pieces. This is as true with multiplication as with other operations.

It is also important for students to realize that when you add, you combine only "like" digits, but not when you multiply. This is a function of the properties of the addition and multiplication operations. To bring out these ideas, you might ask questions like these:

- When you add 45 + 23, why might you add the 4 tens and 2 tens, the 5 ones and 3 ones, and then put the pieces together? How does that make the question easier?
- When you multiply 3 × 45, why don't you just multiply the 3 × 5 and stick a 4 in front, or the 3 × 4 and stick a 5 on the end?
- Why would someone say that 3 × 45 is actually 3 × 40 + 3 × 5? Is it also 3 × 30 + 3 × 15? How else could you decompose 45 to do the multiplication?
- When you multiply 235 × 8, how could you break up 235 to help you? How might you break up 8 to help you?

Task 2

- What do you think of Erica's strategy for dividing 152 by 4?

$$152 = 120 + 32$$
$$\text{So } 152 \div 4 = (120 \div 4) + (32 \div 4)$$
$$= 30 + 8$$
$$= 38$$

- How do you think Erica would use that strategy to divide 2246 by 6? Why do you think that?

Ideally, students will realize that Erica's strategy makes sense since you can put 120 of the 152 items into 4 groups and the rest of 152 (32) into those 4 groups and figure out the size of each group.

Success Criteria

☐ I explain what is right or wrong about Erica's strategy or why it is useful or not.

☐ I tell how I think Erica would do 2246 ÷ 6 and why I think that.

Student Sample with Feedback

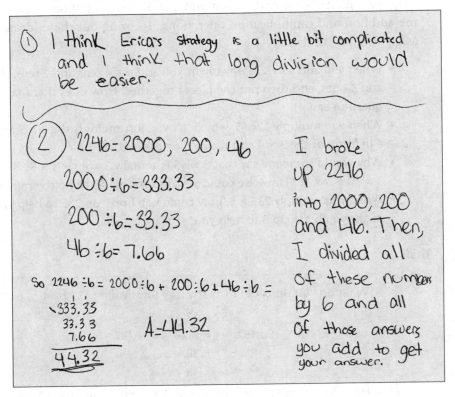

This student seems to realize that Erica broke up the number and divided it into parts before dividing, but missed the point that the decomposition is not about place value as much as it is about decomposing into parts that are easily divided by, in this case, 6. Feedback should acknowledge what she did see but query whether she can see that a different decomposition might have been more helpful. So you might ask:

- Why do you think Erica wrote 152 as 120 + 32 instead of as 100 + 52 when she broke up 152?
- Could a different way of breaking up 2246 have made the divisions easier? Would the answer be different?

You might choose to give feedback about the incorrect addition at the end, but you might well choose to focus only on the decomposition at this point, since that was your learning goal focus for this task.

Another Student Sample with Feedback

> I think Erica's strategy would be almost the same because it's simpler to break it down into small chunks and add, then to try and divide a very large number.
>
> ---
>
> 2246 =
>
> 1800 ÷ 6 = 300
> 420 ÷ 6 = 70
> 24 ÷ 6 = 4
> 2 ÷ 6 = 0.33
>
> 300.00
> 070.00
> + 004.00
> 000.33
> ———
> 374.33
>
> 2246 ÷ 6 = 374.33

This student clearly got the point of decomposing into useful parts, in this case each divisible by 6. But you could help the student extend by asking:

- Would you have decomposed 2246 the same way to divide by 8 instead of 6? If not, what would you have done instead?

Task 3

- Zeke added a number _ _ 9 to _ 8 _ using the standard algorithm, and the result in the tens place was 5 and in the thousands place was 1. Both numbers were more than 100.
- What addition might he have done?
- Describe how you figured it out.

Ideally, students will realize that to get a 5 in the tens place, the first number's tens place must be 6 if the ones digit of the second number is more than 0 or the first number's tens place must be 7 if the ones digit of the second number is 0. As well, the sum of the two hundreds digits must be greater than 8.

Success Criteria

☐ I create an addition of two numbers of the forms _ _ 9 and _ 8 _ where the answer is 1_5_.

☐ I tell how I did it.

Student Sample with Feedback

This student got a correct response, but his explanation of the process is not very revealing. All he says is that he tried numbers until it worked. His process might have been insightful, but you just don't know. So you might ask:

- Which of the digits that you were not given did you decide on first? Why that one?
- What did you do to make sure you had the 5 digit in the sum that you needed?
- What did you do to make sure you had the 1 digit in the sum that you needed?

Another Student Sample with Feedback

First I started off by adding in somthing over the nine as this would affect the tens position.

9 + 2 = 11

| - - 9 |
| + - 8 2 |

Then when I looked at the 8 in the tens position and added the excess 10 from 9 + 2, I needed to add a number that would make 9 a 5. So I put a six

9 + 6 = 15

| _6 9 |
| + _8 2 |
| 5 1 |

⟩ more on back

Then I got the key number 5 in the tens position. From there on all I needed was two numbers that added up equaled more than 1 thousand,

6 + 7 = 13
add the
exess hundred
1400

| 6 6 9 |
| + 7 8 2 |
| 1451 |

69
+ 82
151 ← Key

669
+ 782
1451 ← Key

This student was clearly much more thorough in her explanation. But she, too, should get feedback. You might suggest:

- Thank you for giving me so much information. Tell me why you decided to start at the right first rather than the left. Could you have started at the left?

Task 4

> You subtract one 4-digit number from another one. How many digits could be in the answer? Explain by using examples.

Ideally, students will realize that there could be a 1-digit, 2-digit, 3-digit, or 4-digit answer, depending on how far apart the two numbers are. For example, 9000 – 2000 produces a 4-digit result, 9000 – 8800 produces a 3-digit result, 9000 – 8990 produces a 2-digit result, and 9000 – 8999 produces a 1-digit result.

Success Criteria

☐ I say all the possible numbers of digits that an answer could have if you subtract two 4-digit numbers.

☐ I use good examples to show my thinking and I subtract correctly each time.

Suggestions About What to Look For and How to Follow Up

Some students will not recognize that the difference is really about how close together the numbers are, so you get a big difference when numbers are very far apart and a little difference when they are close together. You might ask questions like these:

- Why is 50 – 49 so much smaller than 50 – 11?
- Could you have known that before you got the answers?
- How could thinking about a number line help you figure out how to get a large answer or a small answer when you subtract?
- How could thinking about a number line help you figure out how to get a subtraction answer of, for example, 1000 or 100 or 10?

Task 5

> A 4-digit number has two 3s in it. One of the 3s is worth 100 times as much as the other 3. What is the smallest number it could be? What is the greatest?

Ideally, students will realize that the two 3 digits need to be separated by a column. So numbers like 3_3_ are possible, as are numbers like _3_3. That means the greatest is 9393 and the least is 1303.

Success Criteria

☐ I create some 4-digit numbers with two 3 digits in them.
☐ I make sure that one of the 3 digits is worth 100 times as much as the other.
☐ I figure out which is the greatest and which is the least of the possible numbers.

Suggestions About What to Look For and How to Follow Up

Many students correctly trade 10 of a unit for 1 of a bigger unit (e.g., 10 tens for 1 hundred, or 1 thousand for 10 hundreds) when they add and subtract, but don't fully recognize why we use the term place value and how it's really about how a digit means a different thing depending on where in the number it is. To bring this out, you might ask:

- Why would somebody say that the 5s in 5055 are really not all the same?
- Why is the difference between the values of the 8s in 8558 greater than the difference between the values of the 5s?
- Why do you think people call our system a place value system?
- Why do you think we only need the digits 0–9 (that's only 10 digits) to show numbers even as big as a million?

For figuring out the smallest and greatest numbers to meet various conditions, students need to realize that the greatest digits possible should be used (i.e., 9s) at the left to get a high number and the smallest digits possible at the left to get a low number. So you might ask questions like these:

- What would you do to make ☐7 > ☐9?
- What would you do to make ☐7 < ☐9?
- How could you make ☐7 as great as possible?
- How could you make ☐7 as small as possible?

To focus directly on the values of digits and to see if students think "multiplicatively," you might ask:

- How much more is the first 7 in 717 worth compared to the last 7?

Although it is totally correct to say that 700 is 693 more than 7, it is probably a more sophisticated response for students to say that 700 is 100 of the 7.

ASSESSMENT AS LEARNING

By learning to self-assess, students can more easily measure their own understanding and make adjustments in their work if necessary. They can gain this important skill by practicing regularly, with peer and teacher support, and using techniques (described in Chapter 2) such as success criteria, rubrics, samples, and self-assessment templates.

In this focus on number and operations in base ten, success criteria attached to particular tasks described in the preceding section would be particularly relevant.

ASSESSMENT OF LEARNING

Assessment of learning begins with a teacher's decision about which ideas, skills, and mathematical practices are to be monitored, depending on curriculum standards that need to be met. The assessment tools that follow address the content standards and mathematical practice standard described at the beginning of this chapter.

Examples of skill questions, concept questions, a performance task (with rubric), and an observation checklist are provided. For each of these forms of assessment, there are, of course, many possible choices; here I provide simply a sampling of appropriate options. A teacher might use some, but not all, of these tools or individual items. Which are used depends on whether observations have left the teacher unsure about student skills or understandings in particular areas.

Skill Questions

Place Value

1. What is the value of the 4 in 4213? In 3416?
2. How would you write 4007 in expanded form?
3. Use a > or < symbol to make each of these true:
   a. 4124   5103
   b. 4124   987
   c. 3906   3888
   d. 457   489
4. Round each of these numbers to the nearest ten and then to the nearest hundred:

	Number	Nearest Ten	Nearest Hundred
a.	458		
b.	372		
c.	1008		
d.	5093		

(continued on the next page)

Computations

5. Use the standard algorithm to add these:
   a. 5128 + 4717
   b. 4992 + 853
6. Use the standard algorithm to subtract these:
   a. 5128 − 4717
   b. 4992 − 853
7. Calculate the products:
   a. 5 × 418
   b. 9 × 308
   c. 7 × 5023
   d. 21 × 22
   e. 38 × 49
8. Calculate the quotients and any remainders:
   a. 5164 ÷ 4
   b. 328 ÷ 7
   c. 4003 ÷ 6

Concept Questions

Place Value

1. What is the least whole number you can create where there are two 5 digits and two 6 digits, and where one 5 is worth 100 of the other 5, and one 6 is worth 100 of the other 6?
2. You write several 4-digit numbers in expanded form, but there are only two pieces in the expanded form each time. What else do those numbers have in common?
3. Without just stating a rule, how would you explain why 4007 has to be more than 3□□□, no matter what digits are in the blanks?
4. □058 is not that much more than □997. What do you know about the numbers in the blanks?
5. You rounded a number to 3500. What is the least it could be? The greatest? Did you round to the nearest five hundred or the nearest hundred or the nearest ten?
6. You round a 4-digit number to the nearest hundred, and the value of the number goes down. But when you round it to the nearest ten, the value goes up. What could the number be?

(continued on the next page)

Computations

7. One of the steps when you add 4129 + 3862 is to add 2 + 6 + 1. Where does that happen and why does it happen?

8. One of the steps when you subtract 5003 − 1814 is to change 500 to 499. Why does that happen and why does it make sense?

9. How are you using the expanded form of 5123 and 389 when you add 5123 + 389 using the standard algorithm?

10. What is a good estimate for 3512 − 2879? Why is it a good estimate?

11. How would you draw a picture or use a model to help your figure out 38 × 48? Tell why your model makes sense.

12. How could knowing how to multiply help you figure out 612 ÷ 6?

13. What calculations do you see in this picture?

	500	30	7
6	3000	180	42

14. How do you know that 57 × 46 is between 2000 and 3000 without even getting the answer?

Note that a number of the questions above deal with the mathematical practice standard related to looking for and making use of structure. Questions that deal with this practice include Concept Questions 1–4 as well as Questions 7 and 8, which call on an understanding of the structure of the place value system. Questions 11, 12, and 13 focus on the distributive property, a structure that underlies how we multiply.

Performance Task

The topics in this strand are varied, so it is unlikely that one performance task could realistically or authentically address all of them. The task provided here focuses on multiplication and division of multi-digit numbers.

- Some computer games are priced at 5 for $219.
- Some tablet games are priced at 3 for $89.
- Using these data, create and solve three different problems that involve division and three different problems that involve multiplication.

A rubric, such as the one shown here, might be used to evaluate a student's success with this performance task:

Criteria	Level 1 The student	Level 2 The student	Level 3 The student	Level 4 The student
Calculating	• carries out few, if any, of the multiplication and division calculations correctly	• carries out some, but not most, of the multiplication and division calculations correctly	• carries out most of the multiplication and division calculations correctly	• carries out all of the multiplication and division calculations correctly
Creating multiplication and division situations	• creates at least one appropriate problem	• creates at least three or four standard, but appropriate, problems	• creates six standard, but appropriate, problems	• creates six appropriate problems, some of which are quite original

Observation Checklist

As teachers observe students throughout their work on this topic, they should take particular note of whether students:

☐ show that they recognize the implications of our place value system in terms of its efficiency and predictability in describing numbers of various sizes

☐ show that they recognize the usefulness of expanded notation in computational situations and also in getting a sense of the size of a number

☐ show that they consistently and fluently add and subtract multi-digit numbers

☐ show that they can multiply or divide multi-digit numbers in a variety of ways and recognize what properties of the operations and numbers they are using in performing those operations

☐ show that they are able to estimate sums, differences, products, and quotients in a variety of situations in flexible ways

Putting It Together

Teachers also have to decide how to weight the various pieces of evidence they have gathered. There is no firm and fast rule, but for a topic that focuses on skills to the extent found in standards in this area, I suggest that weights might be something like this:

Observations	60%	(Observation of both skill and concept work, with a heavier emphasis on concepts.)
Skills	15%	(Additional skill items asked at the conclusion of the topic.)
Concepts	15%	(Additional concept items asked at the conclusion of the topic.)
Performance Task	10%	(Performed at the conclusion of the topic.)

Observations are given the highest weight because they are more frequent and probably more reliable than the other forms of assessment. Notice that concepts and skills are weighted equally in this scheme because standards in this subject area devote considerable attention to both.

SUMMARY

This chapter has modeled what assessment for learning, assessment as learning, and assessment of learning could look like in teaching 4th-grade students the content needed to meet standards related to number and operations in base ten. The illustrated assessments have also highlighted a mathematical practice standard for looking for and making use of structure.

At this level, work in number and operations in base ten focuses on place value concepts and operations with multi-digit numbers.

The chapter features numerous samples of questions and tasks that can be used to elicit diagnostic, formative, and summative data; suggestions on what to observe as students work; and illustrations of feedback a teacher might give. Finally, a suggested weighting scheme is provided for evaluating the array of assessment evidence that can be collected.

• CHAPTER 6 •

Geometry, Grade 5

Assessment and Feedback

THIS CHAPTER explores assessment and feedback in the area of geometry for students in Grade 5. The discussion also highlights a mathematical practice standard focused on constructing viable arguments and critiquing the reasoning of others. While the standards illustrated here apply to the Grade 5 level, other standards schemes might assign some of these concepts and skills to learners one grade higher or lower. Teachers should tailor the information provided to their particular situation.

THE MATH THAT MATTERS

Representative curriculum standards in the content domain of geometry at the 5th-grade level can be expressed as follows:

Geometry

Graph points on the coordinate plane to solve real-world and mathematical problems.

1. Use a pair of perpendicular number lines, called axes, to define a coordinate system, with the intersection of the lines (the origin) arranged to coincide with the 0 on each line and a given point in the plane located by using an ordered pair of numbers, called its coordinates. Understand that the first number indicates how far to travel from the origin in the direction of one axis, and the second number indicates how far to travel in the direction of the second axis, with the convention that the names of the two axes and the coordinates correspond (e.g., x-axis and x-coordinate, y-axis and y-coordinate).

2. Represent real world and mathematical problems by graphing points in the first quadrant of the coordinate plane, and interpret coordinate values of points in the context of the situation.

Classify two-dimensional figures into categories based on their properties.

3. Understand that attributes belonging to a category of two-dimensional figures also belong to all subcategories of that category. *For example, all rectangles have four right angles and squares are rectangles, so all squares have four right angles.*

4. Classify two-dimensional figures in a hierarchy based on properties.

(CCSSI, 2010)

This strand deals as much with the use of coordinate grids as it does with sorting and classifying 2-dimensional figures by exploring the relationships between figures based on their properties.

Tasks and questions in this chapter draw attention to a mathematical practice standard for constructing viable arguments and critiquing the reasoning of others. A common expression of such a standard is the following:

Construct viable arguments and critique the reasoning of others.

Mathematically proficient students understand and use stated assumptions, definitions, and previously established results in constructing arguments. They make conjectures and build a logical progression of statements to explore the truth of their conjectures. They are able to analyze situations by breaking them into cases, and can recognize and use counterexamples. They justify their conclusions, communicate them to others, and respond to the arguments of others. They reason inductively about data, making plausible arguments that take into account the context from which the data arose. Mathematically proficient students are also able to compare the effectiveness of two plausible arguments, distinguish correct logic or reasoning from that which is flawed, and—if there is a flaw in an argument—explain what it is. Elementary students can construct arguments using concrete referents such as objects, drawings, diagrams, and actions. Such arguments can make sense and be correct, even though they are not generalized or made formal until later grades. Later, students learn to determine domains to which an argument applies. Students at all grades can listen or read the arguments of others, decide whether they make sense, and ask useful questions to clarify or improve the arguments.

(CCSSI, 2010)

Using a Coordinate Grid

What do we want students in Grade 5 to understand about the use of a coordinate grid other than simply exercising the skill of naming locations?

Location

One idea is that any location can be uniquely described by two numbers. Conventionally, those two numbers are a horizontal and a vertical distance from the intersection point (called the origin) of two perpendicular axes. However, some students might enjoy exploring whether points can be uniquely named if the axes are not perpendicular, and some might enjoy exploring what other two measures could be used to name points. These latter two ideas are, of course, extensions of the curriculum. What is not an extension, however, is realizing that the order of the numbers naming the points matters for the purposes of communicating to someone else your intended location. In fact, it is just a convention that coordinates are described in the order they are; an alternate convention might have been chosen.

Students should get a sense of how looking at the size of the coordinates of a point can give them a quick sense of whether the point is near or far from the origin.

It is important for students to locate points on a coordinate grid even when the scales on the axes are not 1 (e.g., the x-axis is built on a scale of 2 and the y-axis on a scale of 5). It is also valuable for students to locate points with fractional or decimal coordinates that are not overly complex (e.g., halves or thirds or fourths).

Students should be able to create appropriate scales so that given sets of points can be plotted. For example, they might need to decide on appropriate scales so that (2,5), (18,14), and (35,17) can all be plotted on the same grid.

Describing Relationships

Students should also recognize that sets of points can be used to represent a relationship. For example, if only points where the y-coordinate is 2 more than the x-coordinate are graphed, a line is formed. If only points where the y-coordinate is the square of the x-coordinate are graphed, a smooth curve is formed.

Sets of points can be graphed to model a problem situation. For example, if a set of points is graphed to describe a distance traveled in a given amount of time by a car traveling 50 mph, the point (0,0) has to be included since no distance has been moved if no time has elapsed. The increase in the y-coordinate for an increase of 1 in the x-coordinate has to be 50 to relate to the problem (assuming the x-coordinate describes hours and the y-coordinate the distance in miles).

Relating and Classifying 2-Dimensional Figures by Considering Properties

It is not uncommon for an adult, and certainly a student, to believe that a square is not a rectangle. This is reasonable, given the way very young children learn their shapes. But, in the end, what determines whether a shape is or is not a certain type of shape depends on the definition of the shape that describes its properties.

Since a rectangle is defined to be a 2-dimensional shape with four straight sides that meet at four right angles, a square clearly fits the definition of the rectangle, even though it has additional properties, as well. Any 2-dimensional shape can be named in different ways. For example, a rhombus is also a parallelogram, also a quadrilateral, and also a polygon.

When classifying figures based on properties, students should be aware that there are properties that relate to measurements (e.g., all the sides are equal, opposite sides are equal, there are equal angles), as well as properties that do not involve measurements (e.g., the shape is convex or the shape has 8 sides).

There are also properties that might seem unrelated to measurements, but actually are: for example, symmetry. Line symmetry is related to the fact that points move along a line perpendicular to the line of reflection a certain distance away from the line of reflection on the other side of that line, so length measurement and angle measurement are both involved in defining symmetry.

ASSESSMENT FOR LEARNING AND FEEDBACK

In planning and conducting assessment for learning and feedback, a teacher should be guided by applicable standards. For 5th-grade work in geometry, significant topics have been highlighted in the preceding pages.

To begin, a teacher might decide to administer one or more diagnostic tasks or questions to determine students' readiness for the work to come. As learning proceeds, a variety of formative assessments, both informal and more structured, along with probing or scaffolding feedback, can help keep students on track to meeting curriculum goals.

Here I provide numerous sample tasks and questions, with suggested feedback, as well as an observation checklist (p. 95) specific to topics covered in this chapter.

Diagnostic Task

Use a grid like the one below:

	1	2	3	4	5	6
A						
B						
C						
D						
E						
F						
G						
H						

- Draw a shape in cell D2.
- Draw a shape like it, but not exactly the same, 3 spaces to the right and 2 spaces up.
- Tell how the shapes are alike and different.
- In another spot that is slightly closer to the first shape than the second one, place another shape that has some of the same properties as both of the shapes you drew.
- Why does the third shape belong with the other two?

With this task, you can learn whether students have some sense of how to move on a grid that is simpler than the Cartesian system. You can also see what properties of shapes they think about when given the freedom to choose shapes and properties.

Alternatively, you could use more specific diagnostic questions, such as the ones that follow.

Diagnostic Questions

1. What do parallelograms and rectangles have in common?
2. Is a parallelogram a rectangle, or is a rectangle a parallelogram, or neither? Explain.

(continued on next page)

3. Think about a trapezoid.
   a. How many equal sides can it have?
   b. How many equal sides does it have to have?
4. Use this grid.
   a. Place an irregular hexagon in cell G3.

A						
B						
C						
D						
E						
F						
G						
H						
	1	2	3	4	5	6

   b. Place a parallelogram that is not a rectangle in cell G5.
   c. Place a shape that has all equal angles but not 3 equal sides in the spot 2 up and 3 to the left.
   d. Place a 5-sided shape that has only 2 equal angles in the spot 4 spaces above the shape in Part c.

If you learn, through the task or the questions, that students are simply not ready to think about location on a grid or sorting by properties of shapes, you have to make a decision about what kind of additional work might be needed before moving on to the standards you want to address.

Tasks Designed for Formative Assessment

The tasks described here are a sampling of tasks that might be used for formative assessment of 5th-grade students working in geometry. The discussion of each task includes a set of suggested success criteria that might be developed with students. For some tasks, examples of student work are shown, along with suggested feedback. For other tasks, I offer comments about stumbling blocks students might encounter and suggestions for how to follow up to help them overcome obstacles and increase the depth of their understanding.

Task 1

> All _____s have this property: _____
>
> • Fill in the first blank describing a kind of shape and the second blank with something true about all shapes of that kind.

Ideally, students will recognize the difference between attributes of shapes (i.e., things that are true about particular ones of those shapes) versus properties of shapes (i.e., things that true about each one of those shapes). For example, that one side of a rectangle is a lot longer than another is an attribute, but that it has four right angles is a property.

Success Criteria

☐ I list at least one type of shape, maybe more, and I say something that is true about every single one of that type of shape, not just some of them.

Student Sample with Feedback

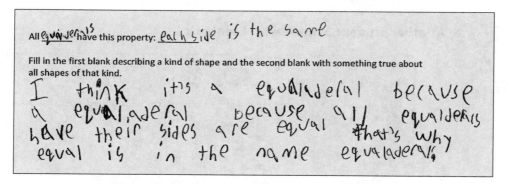

All equivaleals have this property: _each side is the same_

Fill in the first blank describing a kind of shape and the second blank with something true about all shapes of that kind.

I think it's a equalideral because a equalideral because all equalderis have their sides are equal that's why equal is in the name equaladerils

This student has created his own word for a shape type (i.e., "equalateral"), but a teacher would be comfortable understanding what is being said. You might choose to simply let the student know that the term most people use to describe such a shape is "regular," or you could offer a different kind of feedback, such as this:

• Is there anything else equal about the shapes that you are thinking of other than their sides?

• Are the shapes you are thinking of all the same size?

Another Student Sample with Feedback

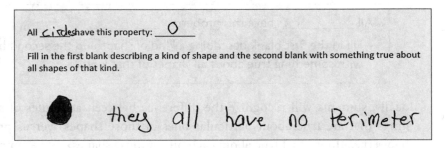

This is a particularly interesting response since it is not likely that too many students would think of it. Clearly, this student has been led to believe that the term perimeter is only allowed to be used with polygonal-type shapes, and, indeed, people tend to use the term circumference for a circle, but is it true that there is no perimeter for a circle? So you might provide feedback such as this:

- What does perimeter actually mean?
- If you created a string that just fit around the circle and made a square with that string, would the square have a perimeter?

Another Student Sample with Feedback

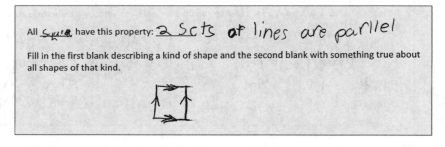

Here the student has provided a great answer. Besides just indicating your pleasure with the answer, you might probe a little more. For example:

- What made you talk about the parallel lines for the square?
- Is a square the only shape with that property?

Task 2

> To move from (*a,b*) on a coordinate grid to (*c,d*), you move up 4 and left 3.
>
> - What could *a, b, c,* and *d* be? Thinks of lots of possibilities.

Ideally, students will realize that the *x*-coordinate decreases by 3 and the *y*-coordinate increases by 4. Some students will actually need to act it out on a grid, while more sophisticated responses will relate the coordinate pairs without even drawing a grid.

Success Criteria

☐ I name lots of pairs of points on a coordinate grid where you move up 4 and left 3 to get from the first point to the second one.

Student Sample with Feedback

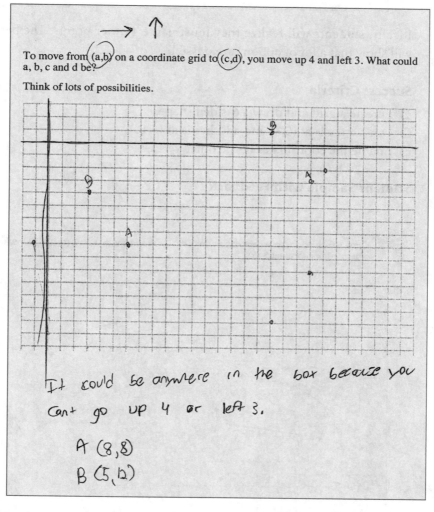

This student certainly showed many points but listed only one possible set of values for *a, b, c,* and *d*. This would not allow her to draw conclusions about how the coordinates change. So feedback to help the student self-correct might be useful. For example:

- So I can see from your work that a could be 8, b could be 8, c could be 5, and d could be 12. Could a and c be closer together? Could b and d?
- Could a and b be farther apart? How would that change c and d?

Task 3

> Draw a 6-sided shape where one vertex is at (5,3) and another is at (6,10). Tell what the other vertex coordinates are.

Ideally, students will realize they must name 4 other points. The best responses will show that a lot of options are possible.

Success Criteria

☐ I create a grid and draw a 6-sided shape.
☐ One vertex is at (5,3) and another is at (6,10).
☐ I name the coordinates of the other vertices.

Student Sample with Feedback

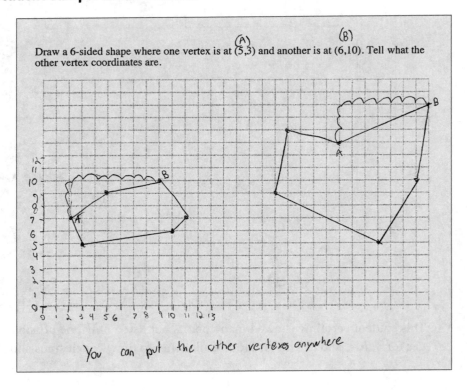

This student did not correctly place A and B nor did he name the other coordinates. He did create a hexagon and did recognize that B should be to the right and up from A. Feedback could focus in a lot of different directions. You might ask, for example:

- Why does it make sense that B is up and to the right from A, just like you showed them?
- Explain how A is at (5,3).
- Explain how B is at (6,10).
- What would you name some of the other vertices that you drew?

Task 4

> You put $8 in the bank every week. But your mom gave you $50 to start with.
>
> - Create a table that shows how much money you will have after different numbers of weeks.
> - Graph points showing (number of weeks, amount in the bank).
> - What do you notice about your graph? Why does what you see make sense?

Ideally, students will realize what the points on the graph represent. Specifically, each point corresponds to one entry in the table. But, more broadly, the first point (0,50) represents the initial value of the bank account. Then there is a y-increase of 8 for each x-increase of 1 since there are 8 more dollars for each 1 more week.

Success Criteria

☐ I create a table that shows the amount in the bank for different numbers of weeks.
☐ I graph the points based on the table.
☐ I describe what I notice about the graph and why what I notice makes sense.

Suggestions About What to Look For and How to Follow Up

Some students will not realize that the initial value of 0 weeks corresponds to the $50 that was already there. So you might ask questions like these:

- If the x-value is 4, for how many weeks have you put money in the bank?
- What if the x-value is 1?
- Should there be an x-value of 0? What would that represent?

Some students might not notice the consistent increase of 8, resulting in a line. To help them see that, you might ask questions such as these:

- How much does the *y*-value go up for an increase of 1 in the x-value? Does that depend on what the values of *x* are?
- What shape do you notice? Why do you think that shape occurred?
- Would the same shape have occurred if some weeks you put in $8 and some $6?

Task 5

> - Draw a diagram that shows the relationship between squares, parallelograms, and polygons. Tell how you know your diagram makes sense.
> - Then draw a diagram that shows the relationship between rectangles, rhombuses, and quadrilaterals. Tell how you know this diagram makes sense.

Ideally, students will realize that every square is a parallelogram and every parallelogram a polygon. They might draw something like:

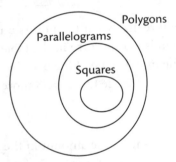

On the other hand, a picture for rectangles, rhombuses, and quadrilaterals would look different:

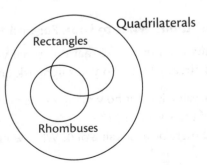

Success Criteria

☐ I draw two diagrams. One shows the relationship between squares, parallelograms, and polygons. The other shows the relationship between rectangles, rhombuses, and quadrilaterals.

☐ I explain why my diagrams make sense.

Suggestions About What to Look For and How to Follow Up

Some students might not have any idea what sort of diagram to draw. To bring this out, you might ask:

- What does this diagram show?

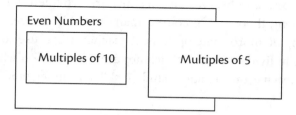

- What kind of diagram might you draw to show that every fraction of the form $\frac{\square}{2}$ can also be written as a fraction of the form $\frac{\square}{4}$?
- Do you remember when we drew Venn diagrams when we sorted things? Would these work here?

Other students might simply not be sure whether and/or why one type of shape is or is not another type. In that case, you might ask questions like these:

- You are looking at a set of shapes. Is it possible that you might call them by one name and someone else by another name?
- Are there some rectangles that are not parallelograms and some that are? Explain.
- Suppose I had asked about triangles instead of quadrilaterals. What about an acute triangle? Can isosceles triangles be acute? Do they have to be?
- Can equilateral triangles be acute? Do they have to be?

ASSESSMENT AS LEARNING

By learning to self-assess, students can more easily measure their own understanding and make adjustments in their work if necessary. They can gain this important skill by practicing regularly, with peer and teacher support, and using techniques (described in Chapter 2) such as success criteria, rubrics, samples, and self-assessment templates.

In this focus on geometry, success criteria attached to particular tasks de-scribed in the preceding section would be particularly relevant.

ASSESSMENT OF LEARNING

Assessment of learning begins with a teacher's decision about which ideas, skills, and mathematical practices are to be monitored, depending on curriculum stan-dards that need to be met. The assessment tools that follow address the content standards and mathematical practice standard described at the beginning of this chapter.

Examples of skill questions, concept questions, a performance task (with rubric), and an observation checklist are provided. For each of these forms of assessment, there are, of course, many possible choices; here I provide simply a sampling of appropriate options. A teacher might use some, but not all, of these tools or individual items. Which are used depends on whether observations have left the teacher unsure about student skills or understandings in particular areas.

Skill Questions

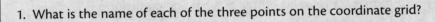

1. What is the name of each of the three points on the coordinate grid?

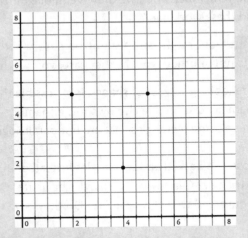

2. On the grid above, place points at (2,3) and (8,0.5).

(continued on the next page)

3. Create a single grid on which you can plot all of these points and then plot them:
   a. (5,9)
   b. (15,22)
   c. (35,4)
   d. (55,6)
   e. (75,18)
4. Lisa created a table of values to show the cost of different numbers of notebooks. Plot this relationship on a coordinate grid.

Number of notebooks	Cost
1	$4.00
2	$8.00
3	$12.00
4	$16.00
5	$20.00

5. Place a check mark *only* next to the statements that are true.
   a. Every rectangle is a parallelogram.
   b. Every rhombus is a square.
   c. Every hexagon has some parallel sides.
   d. Every triangle has three vertices.
   e. Every octagon has eight vertices.
   f. Every pentagon has equal side lengths.

Concept Questions

1. Alison says that if you know the *x*-coordinate of a point, you would know where on the grid the point is.
   a. Do you agree with Alison or disagree? Explain.
   b. How many numbers do you need to locate a point? Why does that number make sense?

(*continued on the next page*)

2. Consider this situation: You are taking a trip that is pretty long. Your family drove 425 km and stopped at a relative's house before continuing. When you start again, you drive 95 km/h.
   a. Draw a graph to show how far from home you would be after different numbers of hours after the stop.
   b. Tell what information is easy to see on the graph.
3. Create an argument to explain why each of these is either true or false:
   a. A square is a polygon.
   b. A parallelogram is a rhombus.
   c. An isosceles triangle is an obtuse triangle.
   d. A square is a regular shape.
   e. A trapezoid is a quadrilateral.
4. Name two properties that have to be true about each shape:
   a. Rhombus
   b. Trapezoid
   c. Regular polygon

Note that a number of the questions above deal with the mathematical practice of constructing viable arguments and critiquing the reasoning of others. Question 1b requires an argument about how many numbers are needed to locate a point and why, and Question 1a requires critiquing the argument of another. Telling what information about the data is easy to see on the graph in Question 2 and explaining why each statement is or is not true in Question 3 also require constructing viable arguments.

Performance Task

The topics in this strand are varied, so it is unlikely that one performance task could realistically or authentically address all of them. The task provided here focuses on the use of coordinate grids.

- You draw an isosceles triangle, a parallelogram, and a trapezoid on a coordinate grid.
- Describe where the vertices might be if the shapes touch but do not overlap.
- Describe where the vertices might be if the triangle is inside the parallelogram, which is inside the trapezoid.

A rubric, such as the one shown here, might be used to evaluate a student's success with this performance task:

Criteria	Level 1 The student	Level 2 The student	Level 3 The student	Level 4 The student
Relating position to shape properties	• tries, but struggles, to ensure any of the shapes have the required properties	• ensures that one or two of the shapes created have some of the required properties	• ensures that the shapes created have most of the required properties	• ensures that the shapes created have all of the required properties
Relating position to positional criteria	• almost correctly positions the shapes in one of the two situations	• correctly positions the shapes in one of the two situations	• ensures that the shapes are almost properly positioned	• ensures that the shapes are properly positioned
Naming coordinate pairs	• correctly names few coordinate pairs	• correctly names a number of coordinate pairs	• correctly names all coordinate pairs	

Observation Checklist

As teachers observe students throughout their work on this topic, they should take particular note of whether students:

☐ show that they can name points on a coordinate grid
☐ show that they can plot points on a coordinate grid
☐ show that they understand why two numbers are needed to describe a location on a coordinate grid
☐ properly show relationships on a coordinate grid and relate the point positions to information in the relationships
☐ recognize that some types of shapes are actually other types as well, based on their properties
☐ recognize that it is the properties of a shape that determine whether a particular shape is that kind of shape

Putting It Together

Teachers also have to decide how to weight the various pieces of evidence they have gathered. There is no firm and fast rule, but for this topic I suggest that weights might be something like this:

Observations	60%	(Observation of both skill and concept work, with a heavier emphasis on concepts.)
Skills	15%	(Additional skill items asked at the conclusion of the topic.)
Concepts	15%	(Additional concept items asked at the conclusion of the topic.)
Performance Task	10%	(Performed at the conclusion of the topic.)

Observations are given the highest weight because they are more frequent and probably more reliable than the other forms of assessment. Notice that concepts and skills are weighted equally in this scheme because standards in this topic devote considerable attention to both.

SUMMARY

This chapter has modeled what assessment for learning, assessment as learning, and assessment of learning could look like in teaching 5th-grade students the content needed to meet standards related to geometry. The illustrated assessments have also highlighted a mathematical practice standard for constructing viable arguments and critiquing the reasoning of others.

At this level, work in geometry focuses on using coordinate grids as well as categorizing shapes.

The chapter features numerous samples of questions and tasks that can be used to elicit diagnostic, formative, and summative data; suggestions on what to observe as students work; and illustrations of feedback a teacher might give. Finally, a suggested weighting scheme is provided for evaluating the array of assessment evidence that can be collected.

• CHAPTER 7 •

Ratios and Proportional Relationships, Grade 6

Assessment and Feedback

THIS CHAPTER explores assessment and feedback in the area of ratios and proportional relationships for students in Grade 6. The discussion also highlights a mathematical practice standard focused on modeling with mathematics. While the standards illustrated here apply to the Grade 6 level, other standards schemes might assign some of these concepts and skills to learners one grade higher or lower. Teachers should tailor the information provided to their particular situation.

THE MATH THAT MATTERS

Representative curriculum standards in the content domain of ratios and proportional relationships at the 6th-grade level can be expressed as follows:

Ratios and Proportional Relationships

Understand ratio concepts and use ratio reasoning to solve problems.

1. Understand the concept of a ratio and use ratio language to describe a ratio relationship between two quantities. *For example, "The ratio of wings to beaks in the bird house at the zoo was 2:1, because for every 2 wings there was 1 beak." "For every vote candidate A received, candidate C received nearly three votes."*

2. Understand the concept of a unit rate $\frac{a}{b}$ associated with a ratio $a{:}b$ with $b \neq 0$, and use rate language in the context of a ratio relationship. For example, "This recipe has a ratio of 3 cups of flour to 4 cups of sugar, so there is $\frac{3}{4}$ cup of flour for each cup of sugar." "We paid \$75 for 15 hamburgers, which is a rate of \$5 per hamburger."

3. Use ratio and rate reasoning to solve real-world and mathematical problems, e.g., by reasoning about tables of equivalent ratios, tape diagrams, double number line diagrams, or equations.

   a. Make tables of equivalent ratios relating quantities with whole-number measurements, find missing values in the tables, and plot the pairs of values on the coordinate plane. Use tables to compare ratios.

   b. Solve unit rate problems including those involving unit pricing and constant speed. For example, if it took 7 hours to mow 4 lawns, then at that rate, how many lawns could be mowed in 35 hours? At what rate were lawns being mowed?

   c. Find a percent of a quantity as a rate per 100 (e.g., 30% of a quantity means $\frac{30}{100}$ times the quantity); solve problems involving finding the whole, given a part and the percent.

   d. Use ratio reasoning to convert measurement units; manipulate and transform units appropriately when multiplying or dividing quantities.

   (CCSSI, 2010)

This strand deals with both ratio and rate, specifically including percent, with a fair bit of attention to solving problems using these mathematical concepts. Embedded in proportional reasoning are two fundamental ideas:

- We can think of one quantity as a unit with which to measure other quantities. For example, we could think of 10 as a quantity made up of five 2s, rather than as 9 + 1.
- Solving a rate, ratio, or percent problem is usually about determining an equivalent rate or ratio that is more convenient in the given situation.

Tasks and questions in this chapter draw attention to a mathematical practice standard for modeling with mathematics. A common expression of such a standard is the following:

Model with mathematics.

Mathematically proficient students can apply the mathematics they know to solve problems arising in everyday life, society, and the workplace. In early grades, this might be as simple as writing an addition equation to describe a situation. In middle grades, a student might apply proportional reasoning to plan a school event or analyze a problem in the community. By high school, a student might use geometry to solve a design problem or use a function to describe how one quantity of interest depends on another. Mathematically proficient students who can apply what they know are comfortable making assumptions and approximations to simplify a complicated situation, realizing that these may need revision later. They are able to identify important quantities in a practical situation and map their relationships using such tools as diagrams, two-way tables, graphs, flowcharts and formulas. They can analyze those relationships mathematically to draw conclusions. They routinely interpret their mathematical results in the context of the situation and reflect on whether the results make sense, possibly improving the model if it has not served its purpose.

(CCSSI, 2010)

Multiplicative Comparisons

The concepts of rate and ratio focus on comparing numbers multiplicatively rather than additively. For example, a ratio of 5 to 2, written 5:2, means that one quantity is $\frac{5}{2}$ as much or $2\frac{1}{2}$ times as much as another quantity. In the picture below, the ratio is 5:2 since there are $2\frac{1}{2}$ times as many dark circles as light ones.

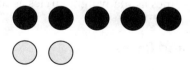

The fact that, above, there are 3 more dark than light circles is irrelevant, since the picture below also shows a ratio of 5:2, and there are not 3 more dark circles than light ones in this example.

Any ratio can be viewed in many ways. For example, I could describe the situation below in several different ways, as suggested:

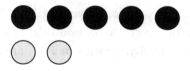

- 5 dark for each 2 light
- 2 light for each 5 dark
- 5 dark for each 7 circles
- 2 light for each 7 circles

Ratio and Rate Language

We write a ratio of 5 to 2 as 5:2. We often write a rate of, for example, $5 for 2 items, as $\frac{5}{2}$ or 5 per 2. When we write 5:2 to mean there are 5 of one kind of item for each 2 of another, this is a part-to-part ratio. When we write 5:7 to mean there are 5 of one kind of item out of each 7 items, this is a part-to-whole ratio. It is important that students realize that any ratio situation includes both part-to-part and part-to-whole aspects.

Although ratios are not fractions, since fractions are numbers and ratios are relationships, ratios are closely related to fractions. Any ratio situation can be described using fractions in multiple ways. For example, if there are 5 dark circles for each 2 light ones, then:

- $\frac{5}{7}$ of the circles are dark.
- $\frac{2}{7}$ of the circles are light.
- There are $\frac{5}{2}$ times as many dark circles as light ones.
- There are $\frac{2}{5}$ times as many light circles as dark ones.

Equivalent Ratios and Rates

Ratios or rates are called equivalent when they are in a different form but say the same thing. For example, if there are 5 dark circles for each 2 light ones, then there are also 10 dark for each 4 light, or 20 dark for each 8 light, so the ratios 5:2, 10:4, and 20:8 are equivalent.

Similarly, if 5 items cost $2, then 10 items cost $4 and 20 items cost $8, so the rates $5/2 items, $10/4 items, and $20/8 items are equivalent.

A particularly useful form of an equivalent rate is a unit rate. In this case, one of the units is 1. For example, 5 items for $2 could be written as 1 item for 40¢, which is an equivalent unit rate. It could also be written as $2\frac{1}{2}$ items for $1 (assuming $2\frac{1}{2}$ items makes sense); this is also a unit rate.

Conversions of measurements involving change of units is all about creating equivalent ratios. For example, converting $3\frac{1}{2}$ feet to inches involves using the ratio 1:12 for feet to inches to create the equivalent ratio $3\frac{1}{2}$:42.

Most problems involving ratios or rates are solved by using equivalent ratios or rates.

Representing Ratios and Rates

Ratios and their equivalents can be represented in many ways, including by using ratio tables, graphs, tape diagrams, and double number lines. Each representation makes equivalent ratios visible. It is important that students see the relationships between the various representations.

Ratio Tables

A ratio table is an organized way to show equivalent ratios. For example, the table below indicates that 50:1 = 100:2 = 200:4 = 1000:20:

First term	50	100	200	1000
Second term	1	2	4	20

Students should realize that any column could be multiplied or divided by any non-zero value to get another equivalent ratio, or another column, in the table. Students should also come to understand why columns in a ratio table can be added or subtracted to create equivalent ratios (Small, 2015).

Graphs

A rate can be plotted on a graph to show equivalent forms of that rate. The graph below makes it easy to see that 50 miles per hour (which can also be written 50 mph or 50 miles/h) is equivalent to 100 miles/2 hours or 75 miles/$1\frac{1}{2}$ hours, and so forth.

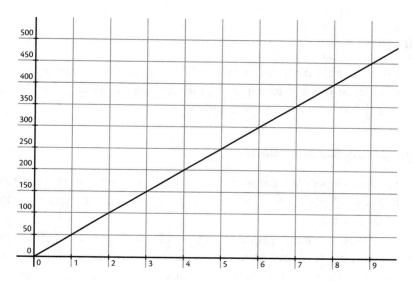

Tape Diagrams

A tape diagram is a visual that shows the relationship between two quantities. For example, the ratio 50:1 might be shown like this:

1		1		1	
50		50		50	

The equivalent ratios are not as obvious in the tape diagram as in the graph or ratio table, but they are inherent in a tape diagram. For example, using two copies of the 1:50 relationship shows a total of 2:100.

Double Number Lines

A double number line can also be used to show ratios. For a ratio of 50:1, the value 50 on one line corresponds with the value 1 on the other. Equivalent ratios are based on the two scales on the two number lines.

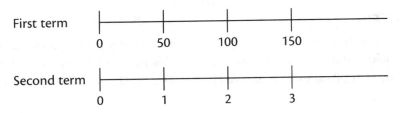

Percents

Percents are a particular way of writing equivalent ratios by forcing the second term to be 100. For example, the ratio 5:6 is equivalent to 10:12 or 60:72, but also to $83\frac{1}{3}$:100, so it can be expressed as 83.33...%.

Comparing Rates or Ratios

Sometimes people want to compare two rates. For example, a person might want to know whether driving 123 miles in $2\frac{1}{2}$ hours is faster or slower than driving 95 miles in 2 hours.

There are many ways to compare rates such as these. For example, one of the tools for creating equivalent rates or ratios shown above could be used to make the comparison easier. Or students might work numerically. In this case, they might recognize that 2 hours is $\frac{4}{5}$ of $2\frac{1}{2}$ hours and that $\frac{4}{5}$ of 123 = 98.4. Since the second speed was only 95 miles in 2 hours, and not 98.4, it was slower.

Students might also compare equivalent unit rates: 123 miles in $2\frac{1}{2}$ hours = 49.2 miles per hour, and 95 miles in 2 hours = 47.5 miles per hour, so the first speed is greater.

Just like unit rates are a way to make comparisons, so are percents. That is because just as unit rates standardize one of the measurements to 1 unit, percents standardize relative to 100. For example, a part-to-whole ratio of 5:8 would be equivalent to 62.5:100 (or 62.5%) while a part-to-whole ratio of 6:10 would be equivalent to 60:100 (or 60%), so the first ratio shows a comparison where the first term is a bigger part of the whole.

Solving Problems

When students solve problems involving rates, ratios, or percents, they are almost always seeking a rate or ratio that is equivalent to the given one.

For example, if you know it takes $2\frac{1}{2}$ cups of flour to make 12 cupcakes and you want to know how much flour is needed for 15 cupcakes, you are seeking a ratio equivalent to $2\frac{1}{2}$:12 where the second term is 15. If you know you can buy 4 items for \$4.75 and want to know the price of 6 items, you are seeking a rate equivalent to 4/\$4.75, where the first term is 6 rather than 4. If you want to figure out the original price of an item that you paid \$45 for at 80% of that original price, you are seeking an equivalent to 80:100 where the first term is 45.

ASSESSMENT FOR LEARNING AND FEEDBACK

In planning and conducting assessment for learning and feedback, a teacher should be guided by applicable standards. For 6th-grade work in ratios and proportional relationships, significant topics have been highlighted in the preceding pages.

To begin, a teacher might decide to administer one or more diagnostic tasks or questions to determine students' readiness for the work to come. In the case of proportional reasoning, students' ability to multiply and divide, as well as their understanding of equivalent fractions, is fairly fundamental to their making sense of what is to be taught.

As learning proceeds, a variety of formative assessments, both informal and more structured, along with probing or scaffolding feedback, can help keep students on track to meeting curriculum goals.

Here I provide numerous sample tasks and questions, with suggested feedback, as well as an observation checklist (p. 115) specific to topics covered in this chapter.

Diagnostic Task

- Calculate each of these:
  - 140 ÷ 2
  - 420 ÷ 6
  - 840 ÷ 12
- What do you notice?
- Can you explain why it happened?
- How is this related to equivalent fractions?

With this task, you can learn whether students recognize that $140 \div 2$ is equivalent to $\frac{140}{2}$, which is equivalent to $\frac{420}{6}$, which is $420 \div 6$, as well as $\frac{840}{12}$, which is $840 \div 12$, and more importantly why it makes sense. Students might appeal to the relationship between fractions and division and talk about equivalent fractions. Or, even more likely, they might realize that if there are 3 times as many people sharing 3 times as much material, or 2 times as many people sharing 2 times as much material, the shares remain the same. Or they might recognize that the number of 2s in 140 has to be the same as the number of 6s in 3 times as much or the number of 12s in twice as much as that. This is what proportional reasoning depends on.

Alternatively, you could determine students' level of knowledge by using more specific diagnostic questions that separately address equivalent fractions and the ability to multiply and divide. Examples of such questions follow.

Diagnostic Questions

1. Calculate each product or quotient:
   a. 45×3
   b. 128×4
   c. 145×10
   d. $412 \div 2$
   e. $837 \div 3$
   d. $512 \div 9$
2. Create three equivalent fractions for each:
   a. $\frac{56}{100}$
   b. $\frac{13}{35}$
   c. $\frac{8}{52}$
3. Draw a picture that helps explain why two of your fractions for Question 2a are equivalent.

If you learn, through the task or the questions, that students are simply not ready to think about proportional reasoning because multiplication or division or work with equivalent fractions is a struggle, you have to make a decision about what kind of additional work might be needed before moving on to the standards you want to address.

Tasks Designed for Formative Assessment

The tasks described here are a sampling of tasks that might be used for formative assessment of 6th-grade students working with ratios and proportional relationships. The discussion of each task includes a set of suggested success criteria that might be developed with students. For some tasks, examples of student work are shown, along with suggested feedback. For other tasks, I offer comments about stumbling blocks students might encounter and suggestions for how to follow up to help them overcome obstacles and increase the depth of their understanding.

Task 1

> Describe the rate 5 km in 20 minutes in LOTS of other ways that really say the same thing. Make sure to include at least two different unit rates.

Ideally, students will realize that not only can you multiply or divide 5 and 20 by the same non-zero amount to get equivalent rates, but also that you can also change units. For example, 5 km in 20 minutes is equivalent to 10 km in 40 minutes or 15 km in 60 minutes, but that is 15 km in 1 hour, a unit rate. Another unit rate could be 1 km in 4 minutes, which is the same as 4 minutes for 1 km.

Success Criteria

☐ I write many equivalent rates for 5 km in 20 minutes.
☐ I include at least two unit rates.

Student Sample with Feedback

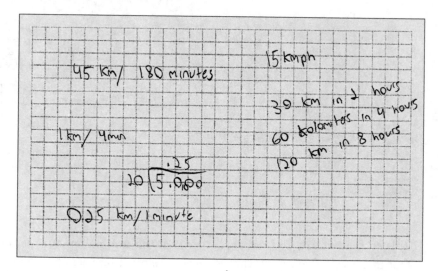

This student has done a great job of using both multiplication and division to get equivalent rates. There are no real problems in the work, although one might wonder why he determined the number of kilometers per minute using decimal division rather than simply using $\frac{1}{4}$ of the 1 km/4 min rate he notes. You might use feedback to extend his thinking. For example:

- Which of these forms of the rate do you think is most useful? Why?

Task 2

> A sale took 30% off the price of an item. You paid $42 for the item. How much did it cost before the sale?

Ideally, students will realize that the original price is greater than $42 and that, in fact, $42 is 70% of the original price. If 70:100 is equivalent to another rate where 42 is the first term, the second term must be 60, so $60 must be the original price.

Success Criteria

- ☐ I figure out the original price for the item.
- ☐ I show my thinking.

Student Sample with Feedback

This student clearly did not recognize that the original amount is the whole and that if she wants to know what is saved, she must figure out 30% of that amount, not of $42. Realizing that the full price was more than $42, she added the 30% of

$42 to the $42. This is a common error, and the focus of the feedback is likely not on why she added but rather on whether determining 30% of $42 is useful. So you might ask:

- You decided to figure out 30% of $42. How did you get the $12.60 in Attempt 1?
- Try subtracting 30% of $54.60 from $54.60. Do you get $42?
- Why do you think that didn't happen?
- Should you go higher or lower than $54.60? About how much?

Another Student Sample with Feedback

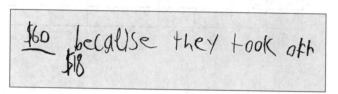

This student clearly knows what she is doing but has chosen not to explain the process. Since the teacher did not ask for the process, the student cannot be penalized for responding in this way. But you might provide feedback by probing for that process. For example:

- I noticed that you said she took off $18. Where did that $18 come from?

Task 3

> Draw a picture that would help you figure out what number 15 is 30% of.

Ideally, students will use a ratio table, a hundredth grid, a double number line, or a graph to figure out that if 30% of something is 15, the whole amount must be 50. For example:

Whole	100	50
30% of whole	30	15

<u>OR</u>

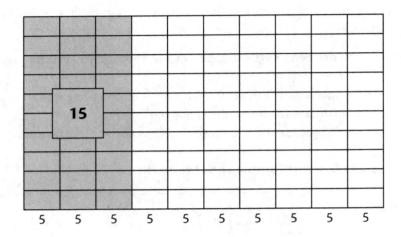

<u>OR</u>

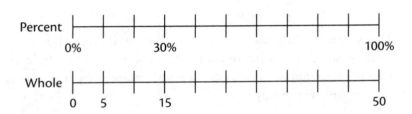

<u>OR</u>

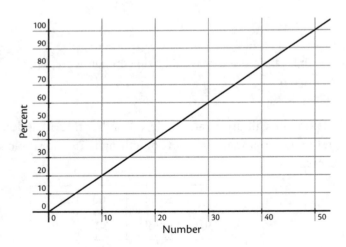

Success Criteria

☐ I draw a picture to show that I know what 30% means and that would help me figure out the whole if 30% of that whole is 15.

Student Sample with Feedback

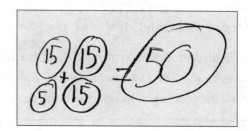

This student recognized that it was essential to use 30% three times and another one-third of that (i.e., 10%) to get the number that 15 is 30% of. The student drew the picture, but did not really explain it. So feedback might focus on that. You might ask:

- How did you know you should put three 15s and a 5 in your picture?
- How does your picture help you see that 15 is 30% of 50?

Another Student Sample with Feedback

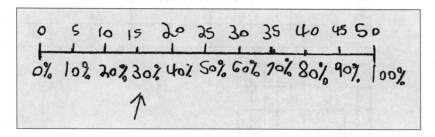

This student drew an excellent picture to help show why 15 is 30% of 50. You might ask:

- How did you know to go up by 5s on the top line, but by 10% on the bottom line?

Task 4

> Show that any number can be 20% of one number, but 60% of another one.

Ideally, students will realize that any number is 20% of the number 5 times as big and 60% of the number that is $\frac{1}{3}$ as big as that one. For example, 15 is 20% of 75, but 60% of 75 ÷ 3, which is 25. So, 15 is 20% of 75 and is also 60% of 25.

Algebraically: That's because if your number is N, and $\frac{20}{100}x = N$ (i.e., 20% of a number called x is your number N), then $\frac{60}{300}x = N$, so $\frac{60}{100}\left(\frac{x}{3}\right) = N$, so your number is 60% of $\frac{x}{3}$. Or you could think: If $N = \frac{1}{5}x$, then $N = \frac{3}{5}\left(\frac{x}{3}\right)$.

Visually: The shaded area representing 20% of the first number uses 20 squares. These 20 squares would be 60 squares if the 100 squares in the grid were each one-third the size, so the whole is also one-third the size.

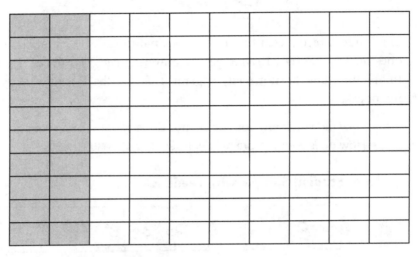

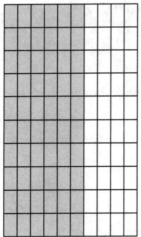

Success Criteria

☐ I show that *no matter what number* I pick, I know what it is 20% of and also know what it is 60% of.

Student Sample with Feedback

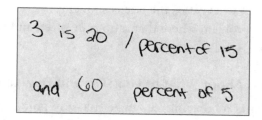

3 is 20 / percent of 15

and 60 percent of 5

This student shows an understanding that the number 3 is both 20% of one number (15) and 60% of another (5), but does not generalize to any number. Feedback might focus on leading to that generalization. You might ask:

- You showed that 3 is 20% of 15 and 60% of 5. What if the number had been 30 instead of 3?
- What if the number had been 4 instead of 3?

Task 5

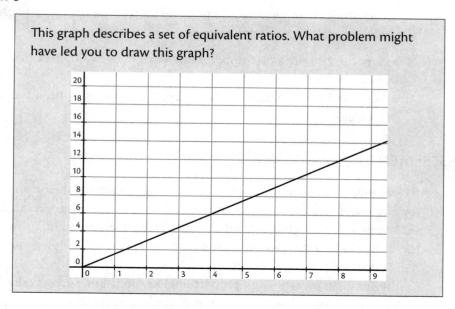

This graph describes a set of equivalent ratios. What problem might have led you to draw this graph?

Ideally, students will realize that the ratio 2:3 and its equivalents are being displayed. The problem could involve a part-to-whole or part-to-part situation involving that ratio. For example, a problem might be: For every 2 bananas in a fruit salad, you put in 3 apples. If you use 8 bananas, how many apples should you use?

Success Criteria

☐ I figure out what ratios the line is showing.

☐ I create a problem where that ratio is involved and where an equivalent ratio might be useful to solve it.

Suggestions About What to Look For and How to Follow Up

Some students might not recognize that any point on the line is an equivalent form of the ratio 2:3. To bring this out, you might ask:

- What are some of the coordinates of the points on the line?
- If you list these coordinates in a table of values, what do you notice?
- Choose one of the points on the line and double each of the coordinates. Is that point on, above, or below the line?
- What if you triple each coordinate?
- How do the ratios of the x-coordinate : y-coordinate of points on the line compare?

Other students might struggle to come up with an appropriate problem. To help them get started, you might suggest:

- Suppose 2:3 were a part-to-part ratio. What does that mean about your problem?
- Suppose 2:3 were a part-to-whole ratio. What does that mean about your problem?

ASSESSMENT AS LEARNING

By learning to self-assess, students can more easily measure their own understanding and make adjustments in their work if necessary. They can gain this important skill by practicing regularly, with peer and teacher support, and using techniques (described in Chapter 2) such as success criteria, rubrics, samples, and self-assessment templates.

In this focus on ratios and proportional relationships, success criteria attached to particular tasks described in the preceding section would be particularly relevant.

ASSESSMENT OF LEARNING

Assessment of learning begins with a teacher's decision about which ideas, skills, and mathematical practices are to be monitored, depending on curriculum standards that need to be met. The assessment tools that follow address the content standards and mathematical practice standard described at the beginning of this chapter.

Examples of skill questions, concept questions, a performance task (with rubric), and an observation checklist are provided. For each of these forms of assessment, there are, of course, many possible choices; here I provide simply a sampling of appropriate options. A teacher might use some, but not all, of these tools or individual items. Which are used depends on whether observations have left the teacher unsure about student skills or understandings in particular areas.

Skill Questions

1. Write part-to-part and part-to-whole ratios to describe a group made up of 8 children and 4 adults.
2. Draw a picture to show the part-to-whole ratio 5:8.
3. Give equivalent rates for the prices shown:
   a. List three equivalent rates to 4 items for $7.
   b. Write two different unit rates that describe a price of 8 items for $16.
4. Write these part-to-whole ratios as percents:
   a. 3:10
   b. 3:4
   c. 5:8
5. What is:
   a. 35% of 48?
   b. 75% of 96?
6. 42 is 70% of a number. What is the number?

Concept Questions

1. What sort of problem might you be solving that would lead you to rewrite the ratio 6:10 as an equivalent ratio?
2. Draw a picture or a graph that would explain why the rates 50 mph and 25 miles/30 minutes are equivalent.
3. The ratio of children to adults at a party is 10:4. Do you know for sure how many people are at the party? Explain.
4. How does changing a measurement of $3\frac{1}{2}$ feet to inches relate to ratios?

(continued on the next page)

5. Andrea knows that 4 cookies cost $1.50.
   a. Why might she have figured out the price of 1 cookie to figure out the price of 7 cookies?
   b. How might she figure out the price of 6 cookies WITHOUT figuring out the price of 1 cookie?
6. Draw a picture that would help you estimate 42% of 38.
7. Fill in the blanks in three different ways to make this statement true: 12 is _____ % of the number _____.
8. Why might it be useful to think of 60 as $\frac{3}{5}$ to figure out 60% of 555?
9. Suppose you know that 14% of a number is 57. What is 56% of that number?
10. The ratio of 11-year-olds to 12-year-olds in a 6th-grade class is 3:2. Two more 12-year-olds joined the class and the ratio became 5:4. How many 11-year-olds and how many 12-year-olds were there after the new kids joined?

Note that a number of the questions above deal with a mathematical practice standard related to modeling with mathematics, particularly Concept Questions 1, 2, 5, and 10. Virtually any percent problem involving determining sale or original prices or any rate problem involves modeling real-life situations with mathematics.

Performance Task

The topics in this strand are varied, so it is unlikely that one performance task could realistically or authentically address all of them. The task provided here focuses on notions of percent.

- One of these statements makes more sense than the other. Which is it and why?
  - *Statement 1:* 90% of the people in the world live in Asia.
  - *Statement 2:* 90% of the people in an elementary school are under 15 years old.
- Now, make up 10 statements that use different percents.
  - Five of them should make no sense.
  - Five of them should make sense.
  - Tell which is which and how you know.

A rubric, such as the one shown here, might be used to evaluate a student's success with this performance task:

Criteria	Level 1 The student	Level 2 The student	Level 3 The student	Level 4 The student
Evaluates the reasonableness of the given statements	• shows little understanding of what Statements 1 and 2 connote	• realizes Statement 2 makes more sense than Statement 1 but not why	• roughly indicates why Statement 2 makes more sense than Statement 1	• clearly indicates why Statement 2 makes more sense than Statement 1
Creates statements involving percents	• creates at least 1 true and 1 false statement involving percents that are fairly similar and are reasonably simple	• creates at least 3 true and 3 false statements involving percents that are fairly similar and are reasonably simple	• creates 5 true and 5 false statements involving percents that are fairly similar and are reasonably simple	• creates 5 true and 5 false statements involving percents, a number of which are quite distinctive and/or complex
Explains the logic of the statements created	• gives good reasons for why one or two of the created statements are true or false	• gives good reasons for why a few of the created statements are true or false	• gives good reasons for why many of the created statements are true or false	• gives very clear reasons for why each of the created statements is true or false

Observation Checklist

As teachers observe students throughout their work on this topic, they should take particular note of whether students:

☐ see more than one ratio in any given situation
☐ see the relationship between, but also the difference between, fractions and ratios
☐ reasonably estimate percents when given wholes, or wholes when given percents
☐ use a variety of tools to create equivalent fractions to solve ratio, rate, and percent problems
☐ use good judgment in deciding when unit rates are efficient for solving rate problems

Putting It Together

Teachers also have to decide how to weight the various pieces of evidence they have gathered. There is no firm and fast rule, but for this topic I suggest that weights might be something like this:

Observations	60%	(Observation of both skill and concept work, with a heavier emphasis on concepts.)
Skills	10%	(Additional skill items asked at the conclusion of the topic.)
Concepts	20%	(Additional concept items asked at the conclusion of the topic.)
Performance Task	10%	(Performed at the conclusion of the topic.)

Observations are given the highest weight because they are more frequent and probably more reliable than the other forms of assessment. Notice that concepts are rated as more critical than skills because there is a lot of attention to concepts in standards in this topic.

SUMMARY

This chapter has modeled what assessment for learning, assessment as learning, and assessment of learning could look like in teaching 6th-grade students the content needed to meet standards related to ratios and proportional relationships. The illustrated assessments have also highlighted a mathematical practice standard for modeling with mathematics.

At this level, work in ratios and proportional relationships focuses significant attention on representations, equivalence, and problem solving.

The chapter features numerous samples of questions and tasks that can be used to elicit diagnostic, formative, and summative data; suggestions on what to observe as students work; and illustrations of feedback a teacher might give. Finally, a suggested weighting scheme is provided for evaluating the array of assessment evidence that can be collected.

• CHAPTER 8 •

Statistics and Probability, Grade 7

Assessment and Feedback

THIS CHAPTER explores assessment and feedback in the area of statistics and probability for students in Grade 7. The discussion also highlights a mathematical practice standard focused on making sense of problems and persevering in solving them. While the standards illustrated here apply to the Grade 7 level, other standards schemes might assign some of these concepts and skills to learners one or more grades higher or lower. Teachers should tailor the information provided to their particular situation.

THE MATH THAT MATTERS

Representative curriculum standards in the domain of statistics and probability at the 7th-grade level can be expressed as follows:

Statistics and Probability

Use random sampling to draw inferences about a population.

1. Understand that statistics can be used to gain information about a population by examining a sample of the population; generalizations about a population from a sample are valid only if the sample is representative of that population. Understand that random sampling tends to produce representative samples and support valid inferences.

2. Use data from a random sample to draw inferences about a population with an unknown characteristic of interest. Generate multiple samples (or simulated samples) of the same size to gauge the variation in estimates or predictions. *For example, estimate the mean word length in a book by randomly sampling words from the book; predict the winner of a school election based on randomly sampled survey data. Gauge how far off the estimate or prediction might be.*

Draw informal comparative inferences about two populations.

3. Informally assess the degree of visual overlap of two numerical data distributions with similar variabilities, measuring the difference between the centers by

expressing it as a multiple of a measure of variability. *For example, the mean height of players on the basketball team is 10 cm greater than the mean height of players on the soccer team, about twice the variability (mean absolute deviation) on either team; on a dot plot, the separation between the two distributions of heights is noticeable.*

4. Use measures of center and measures of variability for numerical data from random samples to draw informal comparative inferences about two populations. *For example, decide whether the words in a chapter of a seventh-grade science book are generally longer than the words in a chapter of a fourth-grade science book.*

Investigate chance processes and develop, use, and evaluate probability models.

5. Understand that the probability of a chance event is a number between 0 and 1 that expresses the likelihood of the event occurring. Larger numbers indicate greater likelihood. A probability near 0 indicates an unlikely event, a probability around $\frac{1}{2}$ indicates an event that is neither unlikely nor likely, and a probability near 1 indicates a likely event.

6. Approximate the probability of a chance event by collecting data on the chance process that produces it and observing its long-run relative frequency, and predict the approximate relative frequency given the probability. *For example, when rolling a number cube 600 times, predict that a 3 or 6 would be rolled roughly 200 times, but probably not exactly 200 times.*

7. Develop a probability model and use it to find probabilities of events. Compare probabilities from a model to observed frequencies; if the agreement is not good, explain possible sources of the discrepancy.

   a. Develop a uniform probability model by assigning equal probability to all outcomes, and use the model to determine probabilities of events. *For example, if a student is selected at random from a class, find the probability that Jane will be selected and the probability that a girl will be selected.*

   b. Develop a probability model (which may not be uniform) by observing frequencies in data generated from a chance process. *For example, find the approximate probability that a spinning penny will land heads up or that a tossed paper cup will land open-end down. Do the outcomes for the spinning penny appear to be equally likely based on the observed frequencies?*

8. Find probabilities of compound events using organized lists, tables, tree diagrams, and simulation.

   a. Understand that, just as with simple events, the probability of a compound event is the fraction of outcomes in the sample space for which the compound event occurs.

b. Represent sample spaces for compound events using methods such as orga-nized lists, tables and tree diagrams. For an event described in everyday lan-guage (e.g., "rolling double sixes"), identify the outcomes in the sample space which compose the event.

c. Design and use a simulation to generate frequencies for compound events. *For example, use random digits as a simulation tool to approximate the answer to the question: If 40% of donors have type A blood, what is the probability that it will take at least 4 donors to find one with type A blood?*

(CCSSI, 2010)

This domain deals with the notion of sampling in order to generalize to describe populations, deals with comparing populations using different statistical measures, and addresses probability applied to both single events and compound events.

Tasks and questions in this chapter draw attention to a mathematical practice standard for making sense of problems and persevering in solving them. A com-mon expression of such a standard is the following:

Make sense of problems and persevere in solving them.

Mathematically proficient students start by explaining to themselves the meaning of a problem and looking for entry points to its solution. They analyze givens, con-straints, relationships, and goals. They make conjectures about the form and mean-ing of the solution and plan a solution pathway rather than simply jumping into a solution attempt. They consider analogous problems, and try special cases and sim-pler forms of the original problem in order to gain insight into its solution. They monitor and evaluate their progress and change course if necessary. Older students might, depending on the context of the problem, transform algebraic expressions or change the viewing window on their graphing calculator to get the information they need. Mathematically proficient students can explain correspondences between equations, verbal descriptions, tables, and graphs or draw diagrams of important features and relationships, graph data, and search for regularity or trends. Younger students might rely on using concrete objects or pictures to help conceptualize and solve a problem. Mathematically proficient students check their answers to problems using a different method, and they continually ask themselves, "Does this make sense?" They can understand the approaches of others to solving complex problems and identify correspondences between different approaches.

(CCSSI, 2010)

Statistics

Statistical tools and statistical measures are used to describe attributes of populations. For example, one might want to know the proportions of left-handed and right-handed people in a group. An analysis might be conducted to learn the proportions of male versus female births for a certain type of animal. A study might be designed to determine something more qualitative, such as the enjoyment of movies, in a certain population.

Statistical tools include things like questionnaires, survey forms, polls, and so forth. Statistical measures usually describe typical data for a population or the variability of spread within a population.

The Notion of Sampling

Often it is difficult or impossible to access all members of a population that is of interest. In that case, it is likely that we use some sort of sampling of the population, ideally a sample that we are confident in generalizing from. The purpose of sampling is always to generalize to the population.

Sometimes, representative samples are used. Using this approach suggests that there has been thought given to the variable nature of the population, and different subsegments of the population are included in the sample. For example, a city might be interested in ensuring that children, working age adults, and seniors are all included in gathering information about recreation services that should be made available. More often, random samples are used. In this sort of situation, each member of the population is theoretically a member of the sample; the actual sample is chosen by using some mathematical randomizing approach to ensure a random sample is selected. This approach might involve numbering every individual in the population and using a random generating digital device to decide which individuals to access.

Mathematicians often consider sample size in terms of populations, that is, deciding about how many individuals are needed in a sample to make the sample likely to appropriately represent the population. The "rules" for this are complex. Suffice it to say, at this level, that larger samples lead to more reliability, but that must be weighed against the cost/convenience of too large a sample.

Measures of Center

Some of the statistical measures used frequently are called measures of center. They describe what is, in some way, a typical measure of the attribute in the population of interest. These are addressed in the Grade 6 curriculum. For example, imagine data were collected rating people's enjoyment of a particular movie on a

4-point scale. Some sample of data was collected, each data point being a number from 1 to 4.

One measure of center is the mode, the value that appears most frequently. If more people selected 2 than any other number, the mode would be 2.

Another measure of center is the median, the value that appears exactly in the middle if the data points are all listed, ordered from least to greatest. For example, if 10 people had been asked to rate the movie and their responses were 4, 3, 2, 1, 3, 1, 4, 4, 3, 2, the data would be reorganized as 1, 1, 2, 2, 3, 3, 3, 4, 4, 4. The middle value would be halfway between the 5th and 6th pieces of data. Since they are both 3, the median would be 3.

A third measure of center is the mean, the value often called the average. It is calculated by adding all data values and dividing by the number of values. It is a way of describing a rearranged set of data with the same total, but where all values are equal.

One of the new ideas in Grade 7 is that if we know all the data, we can know the mean, but if we have to sample to estimate the mean, we cannot be sure our result is correct. The accuracy of our estimate depends on the variability in the data.

Measures of Variability

Several different statistics are used to describe how varied a population is. These are often addressed in the Grade 6 curriculum.

The simplest measure of variability is the range, which describes the difference between the least and the greatest value. For the movie ratings described above, the range is 3.

Another measure of variability is based on quartiles; the second quartile is the median. The first and third quartiles are the medians of the first and second halves of the ordered data. The interquartile range is the difference between the first and third quartiles. This value is viewed as more "stable" than the range since outliers (i.e., extreme values) would have relatively little effect on the interquartile range. Box plots show both the full range and the interquartile range.

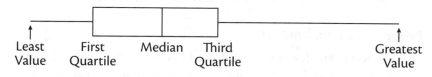

Least Value — First Quartile — Median — Third Quartile — Greatest Value

A third measure of variability is the mean absolute deviation, a measure that describes the average distance of data values from the mean.

All of the descriptions above assume all of the data are known. But if the data are not all known and only samples can be collected, there must be some thought about how many samples and what size samples to collect and how to use them. For example, suppose you want to know the proportion of teenagers who like country music. You can't possibly ask all teenagers. Suppose you managed to collect data from a random sample. You could use that sample's value as your assumed value for the population. But then you might conduct a simulation to figure out how reliable you think that value might be.

Suppose, for example, you learned that 15% of the sampled teenagers like country music. You want to find out how confident you can be assuming that the population percentage is 15%.

You might set up an experiment where you assume the population percentage really is 15%. You choose a sample of, for example, 20 random whole numbers from 1 to 100, knowing that you should get 3 numbers between 1 and 15 out of that 20; of course, that won't always happen. If you do lots of samples, you can create plots to see how variable samples really tend to be. You could explore the effect of changing the sample size, either increasing it or decreasing it, to see the effect on variability, and, as a result, make a judgment on how confident you might be in trusting your sample value based on your sample size.

Comparing Populations

Students at this level need to realize that when comparing means (or medians) of different populations based on samples, there must be some consideration of the variability within the compared populations. If the variability is too great in one or more of the sets of data, it might be difficult to determine which population has a greater or lesser mean or median.

Probability

Probability is a measure of expectation that certain events will (or will not) occur. Probabilities are sometimes based on previous experiences and sometimes based on an analysis of the situation. Probabilistic thinking is essential in exploring the notion of using samples to make decisions rather than full, known sets of data.

Probability Benchmarks

Often events are described qualitatively as likely or unlikely or neither. Mathematicians have decided to describe these situations more precisely by using quantitative descriptions: 0 represents the measure of an event that cannot or will not occur, and 1 represents the measure of an event that must occur. This means that values close to 0 are used to describe unlikely events and values close to 1 are used to describe likely events. Values close to $\frac{1}{2}$ are used to describe events that are neither likely nor unlikely. Every probability is described as a number between 0 and 1.

Experimental Probability

An experimental probability is based on frequency of prior events. For example, suppose that you had asked 20 Grade 4 students if they liked bananas and 15 had said yes. It would be reasonable to say that 15 out of 20 of Grade 4 students (in that area perhaps) are expected to like bananas. Phrases like "20% chance of rain" are experimental probabilities, based on the frequency of rain in the past with similar weather conditions.

Theoretical Probability

Theoretical probability is based on an analysis of the situation being considered. For example, suppose you had a hat with slips of paper—one marked 1, one marked 2, one marked 3, . . . , and one marked 10 (one each for each number 1 to 10). The probability that you will pick an even number is theoretically $\frac{5}{10}$ since there are 5 evens out of a possible 10 numbers and each number is equally likely. This does not mean an even will definitely be picked once in every two tries, but it probably will happen 5 out of every 10 times, over the long haul.

When events are random, the theoretical probability does not change no matter what has happened in the past. For example, if in the situation above, the slips had been 4, 4, 2, 6 in the first four tries, there is still a $\frac{5}{10}$ probability of even on the fifth pick.

Sample Spaces

A sample space is a delineation of all possible results in a given situation. For example, if a spinner looks like either of these, the sample space includes the events 1, 2, and 3. In one case, the events in the sample space are equally likely, but in the other, they are not.

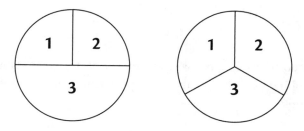

Since probabilities are based on equally likely events, the probability of spinning a 1 is different in each case.

Compound Events

Events are called compound events when there is an interest in knowing about whether both (not just one) events will occur. For example, you might want to know the likelihood of rolling two 3s in a row when rolling dice. Or you might want to know the likelihood that two people carry the same gene.

Simulations

There are situations where mathematicians make predictions of what might happen in a real situation by simulating it with a mathematical situation. To try to predict whether a baseball player is likely to get more than one hit in a certain game, a statistician could use the player's batting average mathematically to calculate the probability he will get one, two, or three hits in his next three at-bats.

Probability Models

A variety of models are used to help people to calculate probability. The most common models are organized lists and area models for single events, as well as tree diagrams for compound events.

Organized Lists

An organized list helps students ensure that they have not omitted any possible outcomes that should be included. For example, such a list for the event of rolling a 2 when rolling a die might be:

Outcome	Number of times
1	
2	
3	
4	
5	
6	

If, instead, the objective was to determine the probabilities of particular sums when rolling two dice, a variety of approaches could be applied. One might be the following:

Die 1 / Die 2	1	2	3	4	5	6
1						
2						
3						
4						
5						
6						

Area Models

Sometimes a geometric model representing likelihood through area can be used to help calculate probabilities.

For example, the likelihood of selecting a prime number from a set of whole numbers under 100 might be shown this way:

Prime   Not prime

The likelihood of getting a pair of evens when rolling two dice might be shown this way:

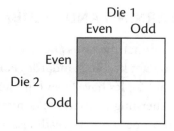

Tree Diagrams

A tree diagram can be used to represent the possible results for compound events. For example, the probability of getting two grays on the spinner shown can be ascertained by using a tree diagram. It is important that each "branch" be equally likely, so the gray is repeated to ensure this.

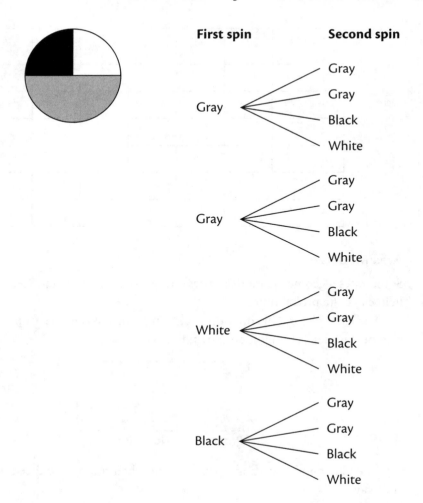

ASSESSMENT FOR LEARNING AND FEEDBACK

In planning and conducting assessment for learning and feedback, a teacher should be guided by applicable standards. For 7th-grade work in statistics and probability, significant topics have been highlighted in the preceding pages.

To begin, a teacher might decide to administer one or more diagnostic tasks or questions to determine students' readiness for the work to come. In the case of statistics and probability, students need to know what means, medians, and measures of variability are and how they are calculated. They also need to be able to compare fractions. A single task might focus on one and not both of these areas.

As learning proceeds, a variety of formative assessments, both informal and more structured, along with probing or scaffolding feedback, can help keep students on track to meeting curriculum goals.

Here I provide numerous sample tasks and questions, with suggested feedback, as well as an observation checklist (p. 137) specific to topics covered in this chapter.

Diagnostic Task

> Create a set of data that meets the following conditions:
> - The median and mean are close.
> - The interquartile range is not too much more than the mean.
> - The absolute mean deviation is about half the mean.

With this task (one possible response: 10, 10, 15, 25, 40, 40, 40), you can learn whether students know how to determine each of the following: the mean, the median, the interquartile range, and the absolute mean deviation. What's more, it reveals whether students can solve problems with these statistical concepts.

Alternatively, you could use more specific diagnostic questions that separately address work with fractions and calculations of statistics. Examples of such questions follow.

Diagnostic Questions

> 1. Calculate the mean, median, interquartile range, and mean absolute deviation of each set of data.
>   a. 17, 19, 21, 22, 23, 23, 24, 25, 35
>   b. 37, 27, 89, 54, 28, 36, 56, 36, 57, 88, 19, 25
>   c. 8, 9, 32, 57, 48, 22, 11, 57, 29, 10, 15, 23, 36
> 2. Which fraction is greater each time?
>   a. $\frac{2}{3}$ OR $\frac{5}{8}$
>   b. $\frac{5}{7}$ OR $\frac{5}{9}$
>   c. $\frac{4}{15}$ OR $\frac{3}{8}$

If you learn, through the task or the questions, that students are simply not ready to think about notions involving comparing populations in terms of variability or mean or about quantification of probabilistic thinking, you might choose to revisit certain concepts before moving forward.

Tasks Designed for Formative Assessment

The tasks described here are a sampling of tasks that might be used for formative assessment of 7th-grade students working in statistics and probability. The discussion of each task includes a set of suggested success criteria that might be developed with students. For some tasks, examples of student work are shown, along with suggested feedback. For other tasks, I offer comments about stumbling blocks students might encounter and suggestions for how to follow up to help them overcome obstacles and increase the depth of their understanding.

Task 1

> The probability of something is $\frac{7}{10}$. What might the event be?

Ideally, students will realize that the probability could be theoretical or experimental. For example, a student might think of a situation with 7 red cubes and 3 blue cubes in a bag where a cube is selected without looking and the question is about the probability of picking a red cube.

A student might, instead, think of a situation where 10 children are asked their favorite color and 7 of them chose either red, yellow, or blue. The probability $\frac{7}{10}$ might describe the probability of choosing a primary color.

Other students might be even more sophisticated and think of a more complex situation, for example, the probability of choosing a red or blue cube from a bag with 3 reds, 4 blues, and 3 yellows.

Success Criteria

☐ I describe an event where the probability is $\frac{7}{10}$ and I explain how I know.

Student Sample with Feedback

Jimmy goes to walmart ten times 7 times he buys baloneys 3 of those times he buys baguettes for his baloney.

This student set up the situation, but didn't really tell us what has the probability of $\frac{7}{10}$. We have to infer his intent. Feedback could focus on that, but more productive feedback might focus on the notion of probability as a prediction. You might ask:

- Do you think the value $\frac{7}{10}$ could be used to predict what happens the next few times he goes to Walmart? What would it predict?

Another Student Sample with Feedback

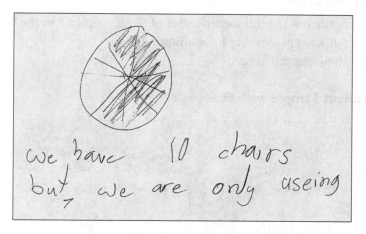

This student chose to represent $\frac{7}{10}$ and described a situation involving $\frac{7}{10}$, but really did not address probability at all. Feedback might focus on that:

- I see the $\frac{7}{10}$ in the picture and in your description of the chairs. What is it about the situation that makes you think of probability?

Task 2

> - You drew a tree diagram to describe the probability of getting a certain color combination when you choose 2 colored cubes from a bag. The probability turned out to be $\frac{4}{30}$.
> - What could the colors in the bag be?
> - What probability were you trying to figure out?

Note that although showing their thinking was not explicitly mentioned in the task, that should be expected of students all the time unless they are explicitly told it is not necessary. That is, students should assume that math normally involves explaining their thinking unless they are performing a straightforward calculation or repetition of a learned process or definition.

In this case, students should realize that $\frac{4}{30}$ suggests their tree diagram needs to have a total of 30 branches, only 4 of which satisfy the necessary condition. They might realize that 30 branches might occur if there are 6 outcomes for the first pick and 5 for the second or 3 outcomes for the first pick and 10 for the second, and so forth. A possible scenario not involving cubes in a bag might involve rolling a 1 or 2 on a die AND spinning a 1 or 2 on a spinner with five equal sections labeled 1 through 5.

Success Criteria

☐ I figure out the number of cubes of different colors in the bag.
☐ I tell what probability I was thinking of.
☐ I show my thinking.

Student Sample with Feedback

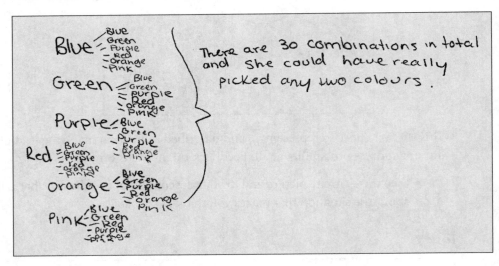

This student clearly has a sense of how to use tree diagrams. Unfortunately, she showed 36 possible outcomes rather than 30. This is more than a simple calculation error because it shows she does not consider that the second event cannot use the same tool in the same way as the first event. Also, she did not really explain how picking any two colors leads to the 4 in $\frac{4}{30}$. You might ask:

- What makes this a tree diagram? Do the second set of branches always have to be the same as the first set?
- Where in your diagram do I see the 30 from $\frac{4}{30}$? Where do I see the 4?

Another Student Sample with Feedback

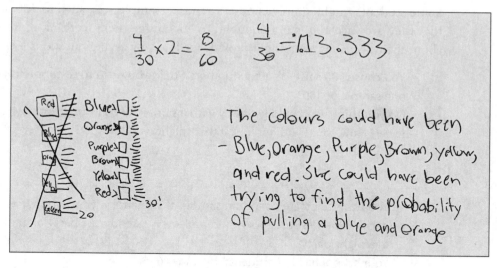

This student recognizes that there needs to be a total of 30 branches. The intention seems to be that the student's second color cannot the same as the first, although that is not clear. Unfortunately, the probability of the blue/orange combination mentioned would be $\frac{2}{30}$, not $\frac{4}{30}$. Feedback might be provided to help the student to self-correct:

- You marked the 30. That's great. Which 4 branches am I looking at for the $\frac{4}{30}$?

Task 3

- You are told that 64% of people in the United States watch NFL football.
- You wonder how big a sample you would need to create to see if that figure feels right.
- How would you figure that out?

Success Criteria

☐ I describe a process for figuring out an appropriate sample size to test the given statistic.

☐ I explain why my method makes sense.

Suggestions About What to Look For and How to Follow Up

Some students might simply choose a random sample size, such as 100, and say that they are sure 100 is big enough. To encourage them to think more deeply about their decisions, you might provide feedback by asking questions like these:

- You chose 100 since it's a big number. Would you need to test more than one sample of 100?
- Do you think you could get away with a sample of 80 instead, or maybe even fewer? How could you find out if that might work or not?

Task 4

> - You want to create a random sample of students in your school to decide whether students would prefer a weekend class party or an overnight party.
> - Your school has 782 students in Grades 6–8.
> - What would be an effective way to create a random sample?

Students need to realize what a random sample is and to come up with a definitive (not vague) way to create one. They should also realize that they have to decide on both a sample size and a randomization technique.

Success Criteria

☐ I tell what sample size I would use and why.
☐ I describe a specific method of how to make sure everyone in the population has an equal chance of being selected for my sample and explain my method.

Suggestions About What to Look For and How to Follow Up

Some students might suggest a rather vague method, for example, "I would pick every 25th person on the list," without explaining how their list was created. You might provide feedback by asking questions such as these:

- How would you create the list? In what order would the people be listed?
- Why did you decide on every 25th person?
- Does the first person on your list have a chance of being selected?
- How do you know everyone on the list has an equal chance of being selected?

Task 5

> How might you create a simulation to decide if a baseball player with a batting average of .286 is likely to get 3 hits in a particular game?

Ideally, students will realize that they can't actually use the player, so a simulation is warranted, and that the simulation has to, somehow, represent the batting average of .286.

Success Criteria

☐ I describe an experiment where the probability is actually 0.286.
☐ I describe what assumptions I make in the simulation.
☐ I describe how to use my experiment to test what I have to.

Suggestions About What to Look For and How to Follow Up

Some students might not realize they made assumptions with their simulation. For example, they might decide that 0.286 is effectively the same as 0.3 (or close enough) to simplify the experiment. They also might make an assumption that a player gets 3 at-bats (at least) in a game without even realizing that also was an assumption. Questions you might ask include:

- How does your suggested simulation use the baseball player's batting average?
- Why would you have to perform your experiment more than once?
- How many times would you have to perform your experiment?
- What assumptions are you making in suggesting this simulation?
- Are your assumptions reasonable?

ASSESSMENT AS LEARNING

By learning to self-assess, students can more easily measure their own understanding and make adjustments in their work if necessary. They can gain this important skill by practicing regularly, with peer and teacher support, and using techniques (described in Chapter 2) such as success criteria, rubrics, samples, and self-assessment templates.

In this focus on statistics and probability, success criteria attached to particular tasks described in the preceding section would be particularly relevant.

ASSESSMENT OF LEARNING

Assessment of learning begins with a teacher's decision about which ideas, skills, and mathematical practices are to be monitored, depending on curriculum standards that need to be met. The assessment tools that follow address the content standards and mathematical practice standard described at the beginning of this chapter.

Examples of skill questions, concept questions, a performance task (with rubric), and an observation checklist are provided. For each of these forms of assessment, there are, of course, many possible choices; here I provide simply a sampling of appropriate options. A teacher might use some, but not all, of these tools or individual items. Which are used depends on whether observations have left the teacher unsure about student skills or understandings in particular areas.

In the statistics and probability strand for 7th grade, most of the statistical work is conceptual and not skill-based; many of the skills are typically introduced in 6th grade (e.g., determining measures of center and measures of variability). However, a teacher might decide to revisit those skills in an assessment, recognizing that they are implicit in the standards for 7th grade. The probability work for 7th grade more directly involves skills as well as concepts.

Skill Questions

1. Describe the sample space of outcomes for each situation:
   a. Getting a prime number when selecting a 2-digit number
   b. Getting a red cube when selecting 1 cube from a bag of 2 red, 7 green, and 3 yellow cubes
   c. Getting a difference of 1 when rolling 2 ordinary dice
   d. Getting 2 red spins on a spinner that is half red, a quarter green, and a quarter yellow
   e. Choosing a pair of teenagers who both like country music from samples of 10 pairs
2. What is the probability of meeting the stated condition in situations 1a, 1b, 1c, and 1d above?
3. What would you need to know to determine the probability in situation 1e above? Suppose you knew that information. How would you use it?
4. Create either a tree diagram, an organized list, or an area model to model the probability of rolling 3 consecutive numbers (in any order; e.g., 1-2-3, 3-4-5, 4-3-5) if you roll a die 3 times.

In addition, Diagnostic Question 1 in this chapter (p. 125), while covering statistics work addressed in 6th grade, can serve as a skill question at the 7th-grade level.

Concept Questions

1. Jennifer thinks that the best way to pick a good sample of 7th-graders to ask about their favorite sport to watch is to choose some kids on the hockey team, some on the soccer team, and some on the track team. Do you agree or disagree with Jennifer? Explain your thinking.

2. Kyle asked a random group of 100 people at the local shopping mall on Monday morning how important they think it is that the mall be open later than 5 p.m. on Saturday. Do you think this is a good sample or not? Explain.

3. You want to estimate the proportion of 12- and 13-year-olds who like roller coasters. You asked 20 different sets of 10 random 12- and 13-year-olds whether they liked roller coasters and your results were: 70%, 40%, 60%, 20%, 70%, 60%, 50%, 30%, 40%, 50%. What conclusions do you think you could draw?

4. You have tossed a coin 7 times. You got a head each time. What will happen next?

5. You pulled a cube from a bag of 12 cubes and returned it each time. The colors in the first 20 pulls were: Y, Y, R, G, R, Y, Y, B, B, R, R, Y, Y, G, R, Y, R, Y, G, Y. How many cubes of each color (yellow, red, green, blue) do you think were in the bag? Explain your thinking.

6. You want to compare the typical heights of 12-year-olds and 13-year-olds. How would you set up an experiment to do that?

Note that Question 6 deals with the mathematical practice standard related to making sense of problems and persevering in solving them.

Performance Task

The topics in this strand are highly connected, so a single task might address quite a few of the standards. One example is provided here; it focuses on using simulations to compare two data sets and implicitly addresses ideas in both statistics and probability.

The approximate distribution of blood types in the United States is:

O positive	38%
O negative	7%
A positive	34%
A negative	6%
B positive	9%
B negative	2%
AB positive	3%
AB negative	1%

(https://www.livescience.com/36559
-common-blood-type-donation.html)

- Create and carry out a simulation to determine how few donor samples might be needed to have relative assurance (no guarantees, of course) that:
  a. Some A negative blood is collected
  b. Some B negative blood is collected
- Describe why your simulation is appropriate.
- Describe your thinking in solving the problem.

A rubric, such as the one shown here, might be used to evaluate a student's success with this performance task:

Criteria	Level 1 The student	Level 2 The student	Level 3 The student	Level 4 The student
Appropriateness of the simulation	• creates a situation very similar to ones already seen that almost embodies the required probabilities but might be awkward to actually carry out • does not draw appropriate conclusions based on the simulation	• creates a situation very similar to ones already seen that embodies some of the required probabilities but might be awkward to actually carry out • draws some appropriate conclusions based on the simulation	• creates a situation very similar to ones already seen that correctly embodies the required probabilities and that can be manageably carried out • draws appropriate conclusions based on the simulation	• creates a situation that is appropriate and unique that embodies the required probabilities and that can be manageably carried out • draws appropriate conclusions based on the simulation

Communication of thinking	• poorly describes his or her thinking in choosing the simulation • poorly describes how the simulation is used	• somewhat describes his or her thinking in choosing the simulation • somewhat describes how the simulation is used	• adequately describes his or her thinking in choosing the simulation • adequately describes how the simulation is used	• very clearly describes his or her thinking in choosing the simulation • very clearly describes how the simulation is used
Appropriate use of the simulation	• carries out the simulation with many flaws	• carries out the simulation with some flaws	• carries out the simulation correctly	

Observation Checklist

As teachers observe students throughout their work on this topic, they should take particular note of whether students:

☐ recognize when sampling is not random and the implications of that

☐ specifically recognize the need, in a random sample, for each member of the sample to have an equal chance of being selected

☐ recognize how the variability in an attribute of a population can affect inferences that can be made when comparing two populations

☐ recognize the need to address both sample size and sample selection in using samples to generalize to populations

☐ recognize what must be considered in determining probabilities of compound events

☐ understand the role of probability in describing a statistic related to a population when the statistic is unknown and estimated through sampling

Putting It Together

Teachers also have to decide how to weight the various pieces of evidence they have gathered. There is no firm and fast rule, but for this topic I suggest that weights might be something like this:

Observations	60%	(Observation of both skill and concept work, with a heavier emphasis on concepts.)
Skills	10%	(Additional skill items asked at the conclusion of the topic.)
Concepts	20%	(Additional concept items asked at the conclusion of the topic.)
Performance Task	10%	(Performed at the conclusion of the topic.)

Observations are given the highest weight because they are more frequent and probably more reliable than the other forms of assessment. Notice that concepts are rated as more critical than skills because there is a lot of attention to concepts in standards in this topic.

SUMMARY

This chapter has modeled what assessment for learning, assessment as learning, and assessment of learning could look like in teaching 7th-grade students the content needed to meet standards related to statistics and probability. The illustrated assessments have also highlighted a mathematical practice standard for making sense of problems and persevering in solving them.

At this level, work in statistics focuses not so much on gathering data but on making sense of what conclusions are safe to draw. The work in probability focuses on compound events and the relationship of probability to drawing statistical solutions.

The chapter features numerous samples of questions and tasks that can be used to elicit diagnostic, formative, and summative data; suggestions on what to observe as students work; and illustrations of feedback a teacher might give. Finally, a suggested weighting scheme is provided for evaluating the array of assessment evidence that can be collected.

CHAPTER 9

Expressions and Equations, Grade 8

Assessment and Feedback

THIS CHAPTER explores assessment and feedback in in the area of expressions and equations for students in Grade 8. The discussion also highlights a mathematical practice standard focused on looking for and expressing regularity in repeated reasoning. While the standards illustrated here apply to the Grade 8 level, other standards schemes might assign some of these concepts and skills to learners one or more grades higher or lower. Teachers should tailor the information provided to their particular situation.

THE MATH THAT MATTERS

Representative curriculum standards in the content domain of expressions and equations at the 8th-grade level can be expressed as follows:

Expressions and Equations

Work with radicals and integer exponents.

1. Know and apply the properties of integer exponents to generate equivalent numerical expressions. *For example,* $3^2 \times 3^{-5} = 3^{-3} = \frac{1}{3^3} = \frac{1}{27}$.
2. Use square root and cube root symbols to represent solutions to equations of the form $x^2 = p$ and $x^3 = p$, where p is a positive rational number. Evaluate square roots of small perfect squares and cube roots of small perfect cubes. Know that $\sqrt{2}$ is irrational.
3. Use numbers expressed in the form of a single digit times an integer power of 10 to estimate very large or very small quantities, and to express how many times as much one is than the other. *For example, estimate the population of the United States as 3×10^8 and the population of the world as 7×10^9, and determine that the world population is more than 20 times larger.*
4. Perform operations with numbers expressed in scientific notation, including problems where both decimal and scientific notation are used. Use scientific notation and choose units of appropriate size for measurements of very large

or very small quantities (e.g., use millimeters per year for seafloor spreading). Interpret scientific notation that has been generated by technology

Understand the connections between proportional relationships, lines, and linear equations.

5. Graph proportional relationships, interpreting the unit rate as the slope of the graph. Compare two different proportional relationships represented in different ways. *For example, compare a distance-time graph to a distance-time equation to determine which of two moving objects has greater speed.*

6. Use similar triangles to explain why the slope m is the same between any two distinct points on a non-vertical line in the coordinate plane; derive the equation $y = mx$ for a line through the origin and the equation $y = mx + b$ for a line intercepting the vertical axis at b.

Analyze and solve linear equations and pairs of simultaneous linear equations.

7. Solve linear equations in one variable.
   a. Give examples of linear equations in one variable with one solution, infinitely many solutions, or no solutions. Show which of these possibilities is the case by successively transforming the given equation into simpler forms, until an equivalent equation of the form $x = a$, $a = a$, or $a = b$ results (where a and b are different numbers).
   b. Solve linear equations with rational number coefficients, including equations whose solutions require expanding expressions using the distributive property and collecting like terms.

8. Analyze and solve pairs of simultaneous linear equations.
   a. Understand that solutions to a system of two linear equations in two variables correspond to points of intersection of their graphs, because points of intersection satisfy both equations simultaneously.
   b. Solve systems of two linear equations in two variables algebraically, and estimate solutions by graphing the equations. Solve simple cases by inspection. *For example, $3x + 2y = 5$ and $3x + 2y = 6$ have no solution because $3x + 2y$ cannot simultaneously be 5 and 6.*
   c. Solve real-world and mathematical problems leading to two linear equations in two variables. For example, given coordinates for two pairs of points, determine whether the line through the first pair of points intersects the line through the second pair.

(CCSSI, 2010)

Tasks and questions in this chapter draw attention to a mathematical practice standard of looking for and expressing regularity in repeated reasoning. A common expression of such a standard is the following:

Look for and express regularity in repeated reasoning.

Mathematically proficient students notice if calculations are repeated, and look both for general methods and for shortcuts. Upper elementary students might notice when dividing 25 by 11 that they are repeating the same calculations over and over again, and conclude they have a repeating decimal. By paying attention to the calculation of slope as they repeatedly check whether points are on the line through (1,2) with slope 3, middle school students might abstract the equation $\frac{y-2}{x-1} = 3$. Noticing the regularity in the way terms cancel when expanding $(x-1)(x+1)$, $(x-1)(x^2+x+1)$, and $(x-1)(x^3+x^2+x+1)$ might lead them to the general formula for the sum of a geometric series. As they work to solve a problem, mathematically proficient students maintain oversight of the process, while attending to the details. They continually evaluate the reasonableness of their intermediate results.   (CCSSI, 2010)

Exponents

Students in Grade 8 are expected to come to understand that we use exponents to simplify the descriptions of very large or very small quantities. For example, we could write $5 \times 5 \times 5 \times 5 \times 5 \times 5 \times 5$, but it is quicker to write 5^7. We could write 4,235,174,000, but it is quicker to approximate as 4.235×10^9 or as 4×10^9. We could write 0.0003427 or we could estimate as 3×10^{-4} or 3.4×10^{-4}. Many students learn the rules, but they often do not realize why we write numbers this way. They should understand that the conventions make the reading and recording of these numbers simpler to make sense of and easier to operate with.

Students need to be able to work with numbers written exponentially. They need to recognize why, for example:

$$5^0 = 1$$
$$5^{-3} = \frac{1}{5^3}$$
$$3^5 \times 3^8 = 3^{13}$$
$$3^5 \div 3^8 = 3^{-3}$$
$$(3^5)^2 = 3^{10}$$

The explanations for these ideas relate to the practice standard involving regularity in repeated reasoning. For example:

$$5^4 = 5 \times 5 \times 5 \times 5$$
$$5^3 = 5 \times 5 \times 5, \text{ or one-fifth as much as } 5^4$$
$$5^2 = 5 \times 5, \text{ or one-fifth as much as } 5^3$$

So it only makes sense that 5^1 is one-fifth as much as 25 (or 5), that 5^0 is one-fifth as much as 5 (or 1), and so forth. And so the pattern continues:

$$5^1 = 5$$
$$5^0 = 1$$
$$5^{-1} = \frac{1}{5} \ (\text{or } \frac{1}{5^1})$$
$$5^{-2} = \frac{1}{25} \ (\text{or } \frac{1}{5^2})$$
$$5^{-3} = \frac{1}{125} \ (\text{or } \frac{1}{5^3}), \text{ etc.}$$

When combining powers, students need to think, for example:

- $3^5 \times 3^8$ means $(3 \times 3 \times 3 \times 3 \times 3) \times (3 \times 3 \times 3 \times 3 \times 3 \times 3 \times 3 \times 3)$, which is 3^{13}
- $3^5 \div 3^8$ means $(3 \times 3 \times 3 \times 3 \times 3) \div (3 \times 3 \times 3 \times 3 \times 3 \times 3 \times 3 \times 3)$, which can be simplified to $\frac{1}{3^3}$, which is 3^{-3}
- $(3^5)^2 = (3 \times 3 \times 3 \times 3 \times 3) \times (3 \times 3 \times 3 \times 3 \times 3) = 3^{10}$

Students who perform operations with numbers in scientific notation need to concentrate not so much on answers, but on estimates of answers and the notion of precision. For example, should $3.4 \times 10^3 \times 3.724 \times 10^4$ be reported as 12.6616×10^7 (the result of exact multiplication of these values) or as 12.662×10^7 (based on the fact that one of the numbers was written to three decimal places) or as 12.7×10^7 (based on the fact that the least precise number was written to one decimal place)?

Square Roots and Cube Roots

Students at this level begin to understand, ideally both geometrically and algebraically, what the square root and cube root of a number is. They should realize that, for example, $\sqrt{30}$ is the side length of a square with area 30 square units. Similarly, the $\sqrt[3]{30}$ is the edge length of a cube with volume 30 cubic units.

As well, $\sqrt{30}$ is the solution of the equation $x^2 = 30$ and $\sqrt[3]{30}$ is the solution of the equation $x^3 = 30$.

Students should begin to see why some square roots or cube roots are rational numbers and others are not. For example, $\sqrt{25}$ is the whole number 5, which is rational; $\sqrt{\frac{25}{9}}$ is also rational since its square root is $\frac{5}{3}$. But $\sqrt{2}$ is not rational. It is hard for students to realize why this is the case since they can get pretty close to $\sqrt{2}$ with a rational number. For example, $\frac{1414}{1000}$ is almost the square root of 2 (it is the square root of 1.999396, which is very close) and you can get even closer with, for example, $\frac{14{,}142}{10{,}000}$, so a student might legitimately wonder if you might eventually get there.

One might argue that the decimal that the calculator gives for $\sqrt{2}$ (1.414213562373095) is not repeating, but how does the student know it won't eventually repeat? The argument is pretty sophisticated and perhaps too sophisticated for some students. It goes like this:

> Suppose $\sqrt{2}$ were $\frac{p}{q}$, where p and q are integers with no common factors
>   (a simplified rational number).
> Then $p = \sqrt{2}q$.
> If you square both sides, $p^2 = 2q^2$.
> Notice that p^2 must be even. That means p must be even (since an odd $\times$
>   itself is odd).
> So imagine writing p as $2r$ (since it is a double of something).
> That means $(2r)^2 = 2q^2$, or $4r^2 = 2q^2$, so $q^2 = 2r^2$.
> That means that q^2 must be even. That means q must be even.
> But we already said p and q had no common factors, so they could not both
>   be even or they would share a factor of 2.
> This means you can't write $\sqrt{2}$ as a rational.

So for many students, all you can do is have them trust you when you tell them $\sqrt{2}$ is irrational.

Linear Relationships

Linear relationships describe relationships that can be written in either of these forms:

$$y = mx + b \quad \text{OR} \quad ax + cy = d$$

Naturally the variable names x and y can be replaced by other variable names.

These relationships are called linear because when they are graphed using points of the form (x,y), that is, $(x, mx + b)$ or $(x, \frac{(d-ax)}{c})$ for all possible values of x, the graph is a line. Students need to learn that linear relationships, when written algebraically, have variables only to the first power.

Representations of Linear Relationships

Students learn to represent linear relationships using tables of values, graphs, and/or equations, and need to see the relationship between those representations. In particular, we want them to see that the values in any row of the table of values translate to a point on the line, and that the equation of the line describes the relationship between the values in any row of the table of values.

For example, consider the following:

x	y
0	1
1	4
2	7
3	10

This table of values leads to a line that includes the points (0,1), (1,4), (2,7), and (3,10), and any two values in a row of that table can be described by the equation $y = 3x + 1$.

In particular, students need to realize that the slope, or steepness, of the line is described by the difference in y-values for a difference of 1 in x-values. The line $y = 3x + 1$ has a consistent slope of $\frac{3}{1}$, or 3, no matter where on the line one looks.

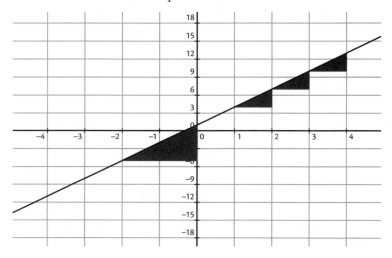

Students should see that right triangles with hypotenuse on the line and a horizontal side length of 1 are all congruent (with the vertical side equaling the slope) and that right triangles with hypotenuse on the line but not necessarily with a horizontal side length of 1 are all similar.

Linear Equations

At this level, students are expected both to solve linear equations with rational number coefficients and to notice the difference between equations that have one solution, no solutions, or many solutions.

Another way to describe equations with many solutions is to think of the notion of an algebraic identity. For example, $2x$ *always* equals $x + x$, so $2x = x + x$ has many solutions and is an identity. Similarly, $12x = 3(4x)$ is an identity. Many students might think of this sort of equation as "simplification." For example, we simplify $4(x + 3)$ as $4x + 12$, so $4(x + 3) = 4x + 12$. Notice that *every* value of x is a solution.

Many linear equations have only one solution. For example, $3x = 36$ is only solved by $x = 12$. Or $\frac{x}{2} - \frac{3}{4} = \frac{5}{8}$ is only solved by $x = \frac{11}{4}$. There is never more than one solution to a linear equation that is not an identity because there is only one y-value for any x-value for the line $y = ax + b$. Below, notice that the only spot on the line $y = \frac{x}{2} - \frac{3}{4}$ where the y-value is $\frac{5}{8}$ is where $x = \frac{11}{4}$.

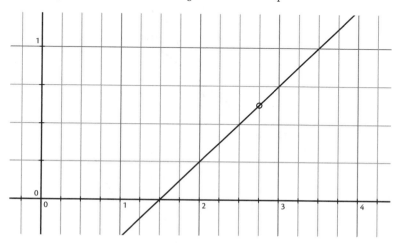

Many struggle with the notion of an equation with no solutions because they don't believe it's really an equation; for them, equations have to have solutions. They would regard a statement like $2x = 2x + 1$ as a lie, not an equation.

Systems of Linear Equations

At this level, students also work to see that there are sometimes particular x-values and y-values that make two different equations true at the same time. The two linear equations involving x and y is called a system of linear equations and the pair of particular values that make *both* true is called a solution.

Geometrically, two lines can either intersect once (in which case there is one solution to both equations, i.e., only one x-value and y-value that sits on both lines), never intersect (in which case there is no common solution), or overlap (in which case the x-value and y-value describing *any* point on that line is a solution). See the graphs on the next page:

One solution

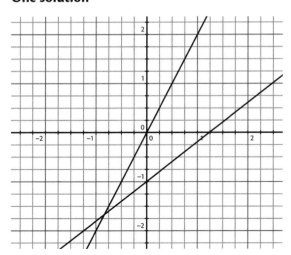

No solutions

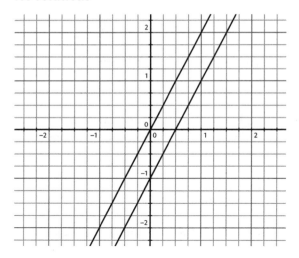

It is hard to see the overlapping lines in a picture, but essentially the same line is described in two ways. For example, $y = x$ is the same as $2y = 2x$, so if those are the two equations, there is really only one equation, and any values where $x = y$ would solve both.

To determine that there is no solution, students need to see that the lines are parallel, but not the same, for example, $y = 2x + 1$ and $y = 2x + 2$ OR $y = \frac{x}{5} - 1$ and $y = \frac{x}{5} + 3$.

To determine a single solution, students at this level are likely to plot both lines using a digital tool and zoom in to estimate the solution. Sometimes the solution is just easy to figure out. For example, if the two equations were $x + y = 5$ and

$x - y = 1$, students might realize that the only two numbers that are 1 apart (i.e., $x - y = 1$) that add to 5 (i.e., $x + y = 5$) are 2 and 3, so $x = 3$ and $y = 2$. This is called solving by inspection. In higher grades, students are often expected to use more formal techniques to solve such systems of equations.

At this level, students also explore problems that lead to two linear equations in two unknowns. Virtually all of these problems put two constraints on a situation and each constraint leads to an equation.

For example, students might be told that they had 52 coins, all quarters or dimes. That leads to one equation, that is, $q + d = 52$. If they are then told that there are 3 times as many quarters as dimes, that leads to another equation, that is, $q = 3d$. Determining how many of each type of coin is solving the system of two equations $q + d = 52$ and $q = 3d$.

There are many such problems students could either solve or create. The focus should be on the notion that there are two constraints and that each is a linear constraint.

ASSESSMENT FOR LEARNING AND FEEDBACK

In planning and conducting assessment for learning and feedback, a teacher should be guided by applicable standards. For 8th-grade work in expressions and equations, significant topics have been highlighted in the preceding pages.

To begin, a teacher might decide to administer one or more diagnostic tasks or questions to determine students' readiness for the work to come. In the case of expressions and equations, students might need to have some understanding of coordinate graphing, including moving between tables of values and graphs in either direction. It is valuable that they have a sense of what an equation actually means and how to solve an equation with at least whole number and perhaps integer coefficients. It is probably not essential that they know about exponents in advance.

As learning proceeds, a variety of formative assessments, both informal and more structured, along with probing or scaffolding feedback, can help keep students on track to meeting curriculum goals.

Here I provide numerous sample tasks and questions, with suggested feedback, as well as an observation checklist (p. 160) specific to topics covered in this chapter.

Diagnostic Task

- You have a rule that no matter what number you start with, you triple it and add 2.
- Create a table of values with these columns to describe a number of inputs and outputs.

Input	Output

- Draw a graph to show your data.
- What equation would you solve to figure out the output if the input is 21?
- Solve it.
- What equation would you solve to figure out the input if the output is 53?
- Solve it.

With this task, you can learn whether students can create and use tables of values to build graphs, whether they understand that equations describe relationships, and whether they can solve equations involving whole number coefficients and constants.

Alternatively, you could use more specific diagnostic questions that separately address skills associated with graphing, with creating tables of values, and with solving simple linear equations. Examples of such questions follow.

Diagnostic Questions

1. Plot these points on a coordinate grid: (−4,2), (1,−5), (0,8), (2,7), (−3,−7).

(continued on the next page)

2. Plot the points in this table of values on a coordinate grid.

x	y
0	7
1	5
2	3
3	1
4	−1

3. Create a table of values that would describe the points marked on this line.

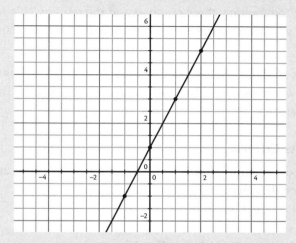

4. Solve each of these equations:
   a. $10 = 3x - 2$
   b. $4x - 12 = -24$
   c. $3x + 2 = -x + 70$

Note that the equations above involve whole number and integer solutions and involve *x* on only one side of the equation as well as on two sides of the equation.

If you learn, through the task or the questions, that students are simply not ready to think about the ideas required by the standards, you have to make a decision about what kind of additional work might be needed before moving on to the standards you want to address.

Tasks Designed for Formative Assessment

The tasks described here are a sampling of tasks that might be used for formative assessment of 8th-grade students working in expressions and equations. The discussion of each task includes a set of suggested success criteria that might be developed with students. For some tasks, examples of student work are shown, along with suggested feedback. For other tasks, I offer comments about stumbling blocks students might encounter and suggestions for how to follow up to help them overcome obstacles and increase the depth of their understanding.

Task 1

> You multiply three numbers and the result is 7^3. What numbers might you have multiplied if at least one is more than 500?

Ideally, students will realize that since $7^3 = 343$, which is less than 500, at least one of the other numbers (or both) must be less than 1. They could be fractions or decimals.

Success Criteria

☐ I use only multiplication and I multiply 3 numbers, at least one of them being more than 500.
☐ The product has to be 7^3.

Student Sample with Feedback

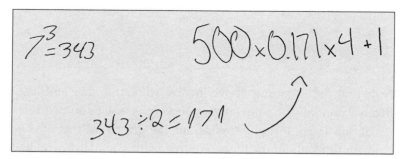

This student shows lots of good understanding. He realizes that:

- to solve the problem if one number were exactly 500, he wants $500 \times \frac{n}{1000} \times m = 343$.
- if m were 4, he would have $2000 \times \frac{n}{1000} = 343$, so the value of n must be $343 \div 2$.

He did not say why he chose $m = 4$ (since he might have chosen $m = 2$ and not needed to divide 343 by 2) and he did make a calculation error in dropping the remainder when dividing. As a consequence, he ended up needing to add 1 to his product, which is not quite what the question said. As well, he used exactly 500 instead of a number more than 500, but that might well be ignored, since it is not critical to showing the math understandings that were at play. Feedback for this student could include questions like these:

- Tell me why you chose 4 as one of your values?
- Why did you divide the 343 by 2?
- Would there be some way to make this work without adding the 1?
- Could two of the numbers have been less than 1?

Notice that the choice was not actually to point out the error in the division, but to leave an opportunity for the student to do this himself.

Task 2

> How are these equations different?
>
> $2x = 50$ $2x = x + x$ $2x = 2x + 1$

Ideally, students will go beyond surface features (e.g., two involve + signs and one does not, or two have xs on both sides and one does not) and realize that a big difference between the equations is that the first has only one solution, the second has an infinite number of solutions, and the third has no solutions. Mentioning the surface feature differences, however, meets the task requirements.

Success Criteria

☐ I say something about all three equations.
☐ I focus on how they are different in as many ways as possible.

Student Sample with Feedback

$x = 25$

visually, these equations are different

because the first one has the number
so, the second one has 2 variables
and the third one has no variables.

Responding to this student poses some dilemmas. There is, of course, an error in saying that the third equation has no variables, although the student is probably trying to say it has no solutions, not that there are no variables. Similarly, the second equation does not have two variables, but perhaps the student means that the variable appears twice on one side of the equation.

So there are semantic issues as well as the issue that the nature of the solutions has not been specifically addressed. As a teacher, you might realize you could have posed the question better, for example, "What is different about the solutions to these three equations?" and offer that clarification to the student. Or you might just live with what you have done and provide feedback like this:

- What exactly do you mean when you say the third equation has no variables?
- What exactly do you mean when you say that the second equation has two variables?
- What would be different about the solutions to these three equations?

Task 3

Graph these lines: $y = x + 1$
                     $y = 2x + 2$
                     $y = 3x + 3$

- What do these graphs have in common?
- Why does that make sense?

Success Criteria

☐ I show all three graphs.
☐ I describe one or more things that are true about all three of them.
☐ I explain why what I said is true is something that I should have expected.

Student Sample with Feedback

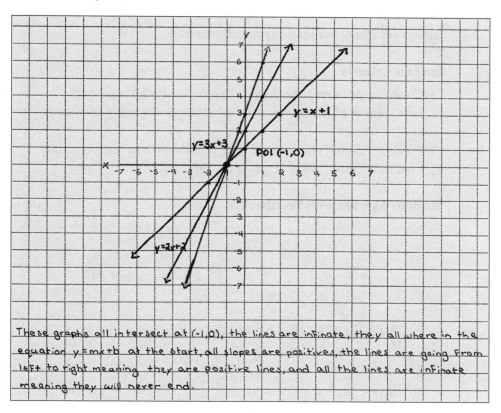

These graphs all intersect at (-1,0), the lines are infinate, they all where in the equation y=mx+b at the start, all slopes are positives, the lines are going from left to right meaning they are positive lines, and all the lines are infinate meaning they will never end.

Notice that this student did graph the lines correctly and did tell lots about the lines, repeating a couple of things in different ways. What the student did not do, though, is explain why what happened made sense. Ideally, a student will realize that if $y = mx + m$ (which is true for each of the graphed lines), then $x = -1$ would have to be the x-intercept since $-m + m = 0$. So you might ask this student:

- Wow—you told me lots.
- Tell me why you might have predicted that all the lines would be infinite.
- Tell me why you might have predicted they all go through $(-1,0)$.

Task 4

> The solution to $4(\Box x + 10) = 3(\Box x + 8) + 26$ is $x = 10$. What values might go in the blanks?

This kind of question might be unexpected for lots of students since rarely are coefficients and constants missing, but the solution given. That might cause some anxiety for some, but certainly not all, students.

Success Criteria

- ☐ I realize that I know the x-value that makes both sides equal.
- ☐ I realize that I have to figure out what the two missing coefficients of x could be.
- ☐ I realize I should check to see if there is more than one possibility.
- ☐ I realize I should always explain my thinking.

Student Sample with Feedback

(continued on the next page)

$$40\left[\tfrac{3}{4}b + \tfrac{1}{4}\right] = 30b + 10$$

∴ the answer in the blank can be any # as long as they're equal.

$$\tfrac{40}{1} \times \tfrac{3}{4}, \quad \tfrac{40}{1} \times \tfrac{1}{4} \quad \tfrac{40}{4} \quad \tfrac{40}{1} = 10$$

$$\tfrac{120}{4}b + 10 = 30b + 10$$

$$-30b \qquad -30b$$

$$30b + 10^{\,-10} = 30b + 10^{\,-10}$$

$$30b - 30b = 10 - 10$$

$$0b = 0$$

when I solved for b, I got 0b=0 so the blank can be 0 to equal each other but each blank must be the same.

Clearly, this student has correctly determined that the first missing coefficient must be $\tfrac{1}{4}$ more than $\tfrac{3}{4}$ of the second one. That means the missing coefficients might be, for example, 1 and 1, or 6.25 and 8, or perhaps $1\tfrac{3}{4}$ and 2. The student actually figured that out, but then went on to say that any value could be in the blank; what she really meant is that if you relate the two missing numbers in the given way, the second missing number could be any value, but then the first number has to be related to it in the correct way. Similarly, the first missing number could be any value, if you made sure to make the second missing number $\tfrac{1}{3}$ less than $\tfrac{4}{3}$ of the first one.

It might be interesting to ask the student for a particular value for one missing value if you give her the value for the other. You might say:

- Suppose you put a 1 in the second blank, what would you put in the first? Could it be anything?
- Suppose you put a 6 in the first blank, what would you put in the second? Could it be anything?

Task 5

I had a system of linear equations and solved it. The solution was:

$$x = 10 \quad \text{AND} \quad y = 15$$

- List a couple of possible pairs of equations in the system and describe how you figured them out.

Many students are likely to go to a graph, plot the point (10,15), draw two lines through that point, and determine the equations. That shows you they know what it means, graphically, to solve a system of equations, and your focus would be on how they actually determined the equations of the lines.

Some students might provide $x = 10$ and $y = 15$ as their first pair of equations, which is correct as far as it goes, but the request was for at least two pairs.

Some students might think more "numerically," and realize that they just need to state some relationships between 10 and 15. For example, since 15 is 5 more than 10, one line could be $y = x + 5$. Since $15 = 1.5 \times 10$, another line could be $y = 1.5x$. So the first pair of equations could be $y = x + 5$ and $y = 1.5x$.

Then a student might consider other possible relationships. Since $2x = 20$, $y = 15$, and $20 - 5 = 15$, another equation could be $y = 2x - 5$. Since $3 \times 10 = 2 \times 15$, another equation could be $3x = 2y$. This makes a second pair of equations: $y = 2x - 5$ and $3x = 2y$.

Success Criteria

☐ I figure out at least two pairs of equations with the solution $x = 10$ and $y = 15$.
☐ I explain how I figure out my equations.

Suggestions About What to Look For and How to Follow Up

Some students who draw two lines might rather roughly estimate other points on the line to determine the equations. To bring this out, you might ask:

- How do you know that that point is actually, for example, (11,16)? How do you know it's not (10.9,16), or do you?

Other students might not catch on to the notion of using the relationship between 10 and 15 to help them write equations. To bring this out, you might ask:

- Why couldn't one of the equations be $y = x + 6$?
- How could that equation change to make it work? (e.g., $y = x + 5$)
- Could it be $y = 2x +$ something? What would the something be?
- Could it be $y = 3x -$ something? What would the something be?

ASSESSMENT AS LEARNING

By learning to self-assess, students can more easily measure their own understanding and make adjustments in their work if necessary. They can gain this important skill by practicing regularly, with peer and teacher support, and using techniques (described in Chapter 2) such as success criteria, rubrics, samples, and self-assessment templates.

In this focus on expressions and equations, success criteria attached to particular tasks described in the preceding section would be particularly relevant.

ASSESSMENT OF LEARNING

Assessment of learning begins with a teacher's decision about which ideas, skills, and mathematical practices are to be monitored, depending on curriculum standards that need to be met. The assessment tools that follow address the content standards and mathematical practice standard described at the beginning of this chapter.

Examples of skill questions, concept questions, a performance task (with rubric), and an observation checklist are provided. For each of these forms of assessment, there are, of course, many possible choices; here I provide simply a sampling of appropriate options. A teacher might use some, but not all, of these tools or individual items. Which are used depends on whether observations have left the teacher unsure about student skills or understandings in particular areas.

Skill Questions

1. Simplify each:
   a. $3^5 \times 3^4$
   b. $3^5 \div 3^7$
   c. $(3^5)^2$
2. Write an expression equivalent to 5^{-4} using positive exponents.
3. Estimate each amount using an expression of the form $\square \times 10^{\square}$:
   a. 57,437
   b. 428,187,100
   c. 0.003875
   d. 0.000041
4. Write the result in scientific notation:
   a. $4.2 \times 10^5 \div 3.8 \times 10^{-4}$
   b. $4.2 \times 10^5 \times 3.8 \times 10^{-4}$
5. Solve each equation:
   a. $x^3 = 130$
   b. $x^2 = 54$
6. Solve each equation:
   a. $\frac{4}{5}x - \frac{1}{3} = 6$
   b. $\frac{2}{3}x + \frac{3}{8} = 4 - \frac{5}{6}x$
7. Solve each system of equations:
   a. $5x + 3y = 56$ AND $5x + 2y = 54$
   b. $6x - y = 44$ AND $x + y = 12$

Concept Questions

1. How would you explain to someone, without just stating a rule, why it makes sense that $(5^3)^2 \div 5^7 = 5^{-1}$?
2. Why is it easier to have a feel for how much, for example, 4×10^6 is than 4,128,350 is? Or is it?
3. You've learned how to use scientific notation. In what sorts of situations do you think it might be useful?
4. What equation does $\sqrt[3]{28}$ solve? Why is it not a linear equation?
5. Why are some square roots rational numbers and some not?
6. What picture could you draw to help someone understand that no matter what two points on a line you use, you end up with the same slope for that line?
7. Give examples of linear equations with the given number of solutions or tell why that number is not possible:
   a. 1 solution
   b. 0 solutions
   c. 2 solutions
   d. LOTS of solutions
8. Give examples of a system of linear equations with:
   a. 1 solution
   b. 0 solutions
9. Why are there lots of solutions to the system of equations $3x + 6y = 12$ AND $x + 2y = 4$?
10. Create a system of equations where the only solution is $x = 5$ and $y = 12$, but you can't use those two equations as your system.
11. When could you look at a system of equations and find it really easy to solve just by looking at it?

Notice that a number of the questions above deal with the mathematical practice standard related to looking for and expressing regularity in repeated reasoning, including Skill Question 2 and Concept Question 1.

Performance Task

The topics in this strand are varied, so it is unlikely that one performance task could realistically or authentically address all of them. The task provided here focuses on systems of linear equations.

> - Think of a real-life situation that would lead you to solve a system of two linear equations in two unknowns. Make sure that there is a solution.
> - Write the equations and solve your system.
> - Repeat with a different situation.

A rubric, such as the one shown here, might be used to evaluate a student's success with this performance task:

Criteria	Level 1 The student	Level 2 The student	Level 3 The student	Level 4 The student
Real-life context	• chooses one or two contexts that are very similar to ones met before • chooses at least one situation that leads to just two equations involving two variables, but there might be no solution or an infinite number of solutions	• chooses one or two contexts that are very similar to ones met before • chooses at least one situation that leads to just two equations involving two variables with one solution	• chooses two contexts that are very similar to ones met before • chooses two situations that lead to just two equations involving two variables with one solution	• chooses two contexts, at least one of which is "original" • chooses two situations that lead to just two equations involving two variables with one solution
Writing the equations	• makes small errors in naming at least one equation that describes the situation	• correctly names at least one equation that describes the situation	• correctly names the equations that describe the situation	• efficiently names the equations that describe the situation
Solving the equations	• makes some headway in solving one set of equations	• correctly solves one set of equations	• correctly solves both sets of equations	

Observation Checklist

As teachers observe students throughout their work on this topic, they should take particular note of whether students:

- ☐ show comfort with large positive, but also negative, exponents
- ☐ have a sense of why some cube roots and some square roots are rational and some are not
- ☐ recognize easily whether equations or systems of equations have multiple or no solutions
- ☐ can reasonably estimate solutions to equations
- ☐ recognize that two equations in a system are really a way to describe the relationship between the x-value and the y-value of the solution

Putting It Together

Teachers also have to decide how to weight the various pieces of evidence they have gathered. There is no firm and fast rule, but for this topic I suggest that weights might be something like this:

Observations	60%	(Observation of both skill and concept work, with a heavier emphasis on concepts.)
Skills	15%	(Additional skill items asked at the conclusion of the topic.)
Concepts	20%	(Additional concept items asked at the conclusion of the topic.)
Performance Task	5%	(Performed at the conclusion of the topic.)

Observations are given the highest weight because they are more frequent and probably more reliable than the other forms of assessment. Notice that concepts are rated as more critical than skills because there is a lot of attention to concepts in standards in this topic.

SUMMARY

This chapter has modeled what assessment for learning, assessment as learning, and assessment of learning could look like in teaching 8th-grade students the content needed to meet standards related to expressions and equations. The illustrated assessments have also highlighted a mathematical practice standard for looking for and expressing regularity in repeated reasoning.

At this level, work in expressions and equations focuses on exponential notation, square roots and cube roots, and solving linear equations and systems of linear equations.

The chapter features numerous samples of questions and tasks that can be used to elicit diagnostic, formative, and summative data; suggestions on what to observe as students work; and illustrations of feedback a teacher might give. Finally, a suggested weighting scheme is provided for evaluating the array of assessment evidence that can be collected.

• CHAPTER 10 •

Conclusion

THIS RESOURCE has modeled what a detailed assessment plan could look like in a variety of content domains at a variety of grade levels. The domains are based on broad subject groupings commonly found in schemes of standards for mathematics. That said, what is modeled in any domain at any grade level 3–8 based on the standards discussed here could be repurposed in a different domain at that grade level or in the same domain at a different grade level using any set of standards that values conceptual as well as procedural knowledge.

While Chapters 1 to 3 focus on broad principles of assessment and feedback in mathematics and, in particular, on how our beliefs about what math matters impact our assessments and feedback, Chapters 4 to 9 provide detailed assessment plans for particular domains at particular grade levels. Different content strands—number, algebra, probability and statistics, ratios and proportions, expressions and equations, and geometry—are addressed, as are different grade levels and mathematical practice standards.

SOME KEY MESSAGES

- What we value in mathematics instruction does and must influence our assessment practice, in gathering both formative and summative assessment data.
- Assessment for learning, whether diagnostic assessment or other forms of data collected during instruction, should be a critical piece of a teacher's instructional plan. Her or his instruction should be informed by the data collected.

    Questions and tasks that are somewhat more open-ended provide more insight into student thinking and might be more valuable for gathering useful data than assessments that are more prescriptive.
- Feedback of different types, whether immediate or delayed, should be provided regularly to help students develop self-assessment skills and foster assessment as learning. Often feedback could be a question, but

it also could be a word of encouragement with a suggestion for further exploration. It is most important that feedback be less evaluative and more focused on the content being explored.

Different types of feedback include feedback that offers the opportunity for self-correction, feedback on choice of strategy, feedback that encourages perspective taking, feedback that is based on an alternative interpretation of the problem, feedback that encourages creativity, and feedback that encourages extension.

Teachers should anticipate and be prepared to handle overgeneralizations, inappropriate assumptions, and other common misconceptions.

- Assessment as learning is enhanced by the use of thoughtful success criteria. This is a way to help students see what type of learning is valued.

- Assessment of learning might include attention to the assessment of skills, but also the assessment of concepts and processes. This assessment might take the form of observational data or data gathered through conversations, but might also involve performances. Often, a performance task can cover a lot of important ground in assessing what students have learned in a mathematical domain.

- Teachers should develop a detailed assessment plan, but should remain open, nonetheless, to unexpected opportunities to gather valuable data about student learning.

INSTRUCTION VERSUS ASSESSMENT

To many teachers, the term assessment means assessment *of* learning. It is critical, however, that teachers see assessment as part of a bigger package, where formative assessment, in fact, plays the bigger role in their assessment schema, and where assessment of learning really just confirms what they likely already know from having gathered data from assessment for learning.

AN ASSESSMENT PLAN

For each content domain, a teacher must take the time to decide what mathematics in that domain really matters, ideally both procedural and conceptual knowledge. What matters should be what is reflected in any instructional or assessment plan.

Once a teacher has decided what matters, she or he might create, for each domain of learning, an assessment plan that includes the following:

- A diagnostic task or questions
- Planned formative assessment opportunities
- Summative assessments that include:
  - An observation checklist
  - Questions focused on procedural knowledge or skills not fully observed
  - Questions focused on conceptual knowledge, including standards of practice, problem solving, communication, and reasoning not fully observed
  - A performance task (where appropriate)

This plan should guide instruction, knowing, of course, that changes can be made based on what actually happens in the classroom.

I LOOK FORWARD to you taking the insights you've gained from this resource to assess the right math in the right ways in your classroom. Remember, too, that giving clear, specific, positive, and ongoing feedback can turn a student around or keep him or her on a positive path toward math understanding and success.

References

Andrade, H., & Valtcheva, A. (2009). Promoting learning and achievement through self-assessment. *Theory into Practice, 48*(1), 12–19. Available at https://doi.org/10.1080/00405840802577544

Barton, C. (2018). On formative assessment in math: How diagnostic questions can help. *American Educator,* Summer 2018.

Beesley, A. D., Clark, T. F., Dempsey, K., & Tweed, A. (2018). Enhancing formative assessment practice and encouraging middle school mathematics engagement and persistence. *School, Science and Mathematics.* DOI.org/10.1111/sssm.12255

Belanger, J., & Allingham, P. V. (2004). *Using "think aloud" methods to investigate the processes secondary school students use to respond to their teachers' comments on their written work.* Technical report for the Department of Language and Literacy Education, University of British Columbia, Vancouver, BC. Available at http://faculty.educ.ubc.ca/belanger/technical.html

Black, P., & Wiliam, D. (2009). Developing the theory of formative assessment. *Educational Assessment, Evaluation and Accountability, 21*(1), 5–31.

Black, P., & Wiliam, D. (2018). Classroom assessment and pedagogy. *Assessment in Education: Principles, Policy & Practice, 25*(6), 551–575. DOI: 10.1080/0969594X.2018.1441807

Brookhart, S. M. (2007). Feedback that fits. *Educational Leadership, 65*(4), 54–59.

Bruno, I. I., & Santos, L. (2010). Written comments as a form of feedback. *Studies in Educational Evaluation, 36*(3), 111–120.

Common Core State Standards Initiative (CCSSI). (2010). *Common Core State Standards for Mathematics.* Available at www.corestandards.org/assets/CCSSI_Math%20Standards.pdf

Confrey, J. (1990). A review of the research on student conceptions in mathematics, science, and programming. *Review of Research in Education, 1,* 3–55.

Cooper, D. (2007). *Talk about assessment.* Toronto, ON: Nelson.

Davies, A. (2007). *Making classroom assessment work* (2nd ed.). Vancouver, BC: Connections Publishing.

Department of Education Western Australia. (2013). *First steps in mathematics.* Perth: Author.

Earl, L. (2003). *Assessment as learning: Using classroom assessment to maximize student learning.* Thousand Oaks, CA: Corwin.

Fazio, L., & Siegler, R. (2011). *Teaching fractions.* Belley, France: Gonnet Imprimeur.

Fennell, F., McCord Kobett, B., & Wray, J. A. (2017). *The Formative 5.* Thousand Oaks, CA: Corwin.

Guskey, T. R. (2003). How classroom assessments improve learning. *Educational Leadership, 60*(5), 6–11.

Higgins, R., Hartley, P., & Skelton, A. (2001). Getting the message across: The problem of communicating assessment feedback. *Teaching in Higher Education, 6,* 269–274.

Karp, K. S. (1991). Elementary school teachers' attitudes toward mathematics: The impact on students' autonomous learning skills. *School, Science, and Mathematics, 91*(6), 265–270.

Kulm, G. (1994). *Mathematics assessment: What works in the classroom.* San Francisco, CA: Jossey-Bass.

National Council of Teachers of English. (2013). *Formative assessment that truly informs instruction.* Available at www.ncte.org/library/NCTEFiles/Resources/Positions/formative -assessment_single.pdf

National Council of Teachers of Mathematics. (1995). *Assessment standards for teaching mathematics.* Reston, VA: Author.

Nicol, D. J., & Macfarlane-Dick, D. (2006). Formative assessment and self-regulated learning: A model and seven principles of good feedback practice. *Studies in Higher Education, 31*(2), 199–218.

Ontario Ministry of Education. (2011). *Initial mathematics assessment—Elementary, Grades 1–8.* Toronto, ON: Author.

Peterson, S. S., & McClay, J. (2010). Assessing and providing feedback for writing in Canadian classrooms. *Assessing Writing, 15,* 86–99.

Principles for fair student assessment practices for education in Canada. (1993). Edmonton, Alberta: Joint Advisory Committee. Available at https://www.wcdsb.ca/wp-content/uploads/sites/36/2017/03/fairstudent.pdf

Rittle-Johnson, B., & Schneider, M. (2015). Developing conceptual and procedural knowledge of mathematics. In R. Cohen Kadosh & A. Dowker (Eds.), *Oxford handbook of numerical cognition* (pp. 1118–1134). Oxford, UK: Oxford University Press.

Small, M. (2015). *Building proportional reasoning across grades and math strands, K–8.* New York, NY: Teachers College Press.

Small, M. (2018). *MathUp.* Oakville, ON: Rubicon Publishing.

Small, M., Crofoot, J., & Lin, A. (2011). *Leaps and bounds toward math understanding, Gr 5/6.* Toronto, ON: Nelson.

Small, M., & Lin, A. (2018). Instructional feedback in mathematics. In A. A. Lipnevich & J. K. Smith (Eds.), *The Cambridge handbook of instructional feedback* (Cambridge Handbooks in Psychology, pp. 169–190). Cambridge, UK: Cambridge University Press.

Texas Education Agency. (2015). *Chapter 111. Texas essential knowledge and skills for mathematics. Subchapter A. Elementary.* Available at http://ritter.tea.state.tx.us/rules/tac/chapter111/ch111a.html

Virginia Department of Education. (2016). *Mathematics 2016 standards of learning. Grade 5: Curriculum framework.* Available at http://www.doe.virginia.gov/testing/sol/standards_docs/mathematics/2016/cf/grade5math-cf.pdf

Index

About the Author

MARIAN SMALL is the former dean of education at the University of New Brunswick. She speaks regularly about K–12 mathematics instruction.

She has been an author on many mathematics text series at both the elementary and the secondary levels. She has served on the author team for the National Council of Teachers of Mathematics (NCTM) Navigation series (pre-K–2), as the NCTM representative on the Mathcounts question-writing committee for middle school mathematics competitions throughout the United States, and as a member of the editorial panel for the NCTM 2011 yearbook on motivation and disposition.

Dr. Small is probably best known for her Teachers College Press books *Good Questions: Great Ways to Differentiate Mathematics Instruction* and *More Good Questions: Great Ways to Differentiate Secondary Mathematics Instruction* (with Amy Lin). She has also authored *Eyes on Math: A Visual Approach to Teaching Math Concepts*; *Uncomplicating Fractions to Meet Common Core Standards in Math, K–7*; *Uncomplicating Algebra to Meet Common Core Standards in Math, K–8*; *Teaching Mathematical Thinking: Tasks and Questions to Strengthen Practices and Processes*; and *Fun and Fundamental Math for Young Children: Building a Strong Foundation in PreK–Grade 2*. She is the author of three editions of a text for university preservice teachers and practicing teachers, *Making Math Meaningful to Canadian Students: K–8*, as well as the professional resources *Big Ideas from Dr. Small: Grades 4–8*; *Big Ideas from Dr. Small: Grades K–3*; and *Leaps and Bounds toward Math Understanding: Grades 3–4, Grades 5–6, and Grades 7–8*, all published by Nelson Education Ltd. More recently, she has authored a number of additional resources focused on open questions, including three editions of *Open Questions for the Three-Part Lesson (Numeration and Number Sense; Measurement and Pattern and Algebra; and Geometry and Spatial Sense and Data Management and Probability)* for K–3 and three for Grades 4–8, all published by Rubicon Publishing. She has created a digital resource, *MathUp*, with Rubicon Publishing, for providing rich instruction for Grades K–8; *The School Leader's Guide to Building and Sustaining Math Success* (with Doug Duff), published by ASCD, to help principals improve math instruction in their schools; and the soon-to-be-released *Understanding the Math We Teach and How We Teach It*, from Stenhouse.